JANE ASHER'S
COSTUME BOOK

JANE ASHER'S COSTUME BOOK

OPEN CHAIN PUBLISHING, INC.

To all children everywhere
who enjoy dressing up – young and old

Photographs by Bryan Wharton

Diagrams by Suzi Bullock

First published in the United States under the title
Jane Asher's Costume Book by
Open Chain Publishing, Inc.
PO Box 2634-B
Menlo Park, CA 94026

Originally published in Great Britain under the title
Jane Asher's Fancy Dress by
Pelham Books Ltd
27 Wrights Lane
London W8 5TZ
1983
Reprinted 1984, 1985, 1986, 1987, 1988, 1991
©Myriad Productions 1983

ISBN 0-932086-31-4

Contents

Acknowledgements   Page vii
Introduction   8

Britannia   11
Firework (or Hayley's Comet)   12
Pixie on Toadstool   14
Ballerina   16
VALENTINE'S DAY   17
  Heart   17
Peter Carrot   18
Harlequin   20
Jester   21
Palm Tree   22
Red Indian   24
Shorter Oxford Dictionary   25
THROUGH THE AGES   26
  Stone Age   26
  Greek   27
  Medieval   28
  Henry VIII   30
  Queen Elizabeth I   33
  Victorian   35
  Twenties   37
  Punk   39
  The Future   39
Knickerbocker Glory   40
Princess   42
Dragon   42
St George   44
Loch Ness Monster   47
Soda Fountain   48
Pied Piper   50
Newspiper   51
Clown   51
Scotch Egg   52
Humpty-Dumpty   53
ZODIAC   54
  Aries   54
  Taurus   55
  Gemini   55
  Cancer   56
  Leo   58
  Virgo   59

Libra   59
Scorpio   60
Sagittarius   61
Capricorn   62
Aquarius   63
Pisces   63
Ladybird   64
Caterpillar   65
Sandwich Man   66
BIRDS   69
  Stool Pigeon   69
  Swallow   70
  Grouse   71
  Jail Bird   72
  Secretary Bird   73
Six Pretty Flowers   74
Daisies   76
Tarzan and Jane   78
The Blob   79
Statue on a Pillar   80
Pea Pod   81
A Circus Tent   82
Samurai   84
Unicorn   85
Submarine Commander   86
Small Butterfly   87
Mature Butterfly   88
Pencil   90
Spanish Dancer   91
Tortoise and The Hare   92
A Portable Galleon   94
Can-Can Dancer   95
Milkmaid, Alice, Bo-Peep,
  Miss Muffet   97
Dr Jekyll and Mr Hyde   98
Teddy Bear's Picnic   100
Minnie Mouse   100
FISHES   101
  Angel Fish   101
  Salmon (Smoked or rock)   103
  Skate   104
  Jelly Fish   105
Red Riding-Hood and her
  Granny   106
Robin Hood   107
Girl Jumping Out of Cake   108

HALLOWE'EN   110
  Bat   110
  Baby Witch   111
  Headless Ghost   112
  Baby Ghost   113
  Nightmare   114
  Witch   115
  Skeleton   116
  A Mummy   116
It's Curtains for Charles and
  Nell   117
Quick Zip-Up Mermaid   119
Good and Bad Fairies   120
A Pair of the Same Suit   122
Judge   124
CHRISTMAS   127
  Christmas Tree   127
  Cheap and Cheerful Father
    Christmas   128
  A Christmas Pudding   130
  Christmas Cracker   131
  A Jolly Snowman   132
LAST MINUTE JOKES   134
  First Class Male   134
  The King and I   135
  Video Pirate   135
  Captain Cook   136
  Steel Band   136
  Florence Nightingale (The
    Lady Of The Lamp)   137
  Alexander The Grate (sic)   137
  The Duke of Wellington
    (The Iron Duke)   138
  Half Nelson   138
  Plato   138
  The Last Straw   139
Papier Mâché Head Shapes   140
HATS   140
  For Robin Hood,
    Pied Piper   140
  Balaclava   140
  For Duke of Wellington   140
  For Nelson   140
Gold Glue   140
Useful Addresses   141

A Note for American Readers

While the measurements in this book are given in metrics, they are easy to convert—if you must. Far easier is to buy a metric tape measure or meter stick and work in metrics.

You need only two measurements to convert:

$$1" = 2.5cm \text{ or } 25mm$$
$$1 \text{ yd.} = 0.9 \text{ meters}$$

Now use a calculator to convert metrics to imperial, and then round off.

Example 1: $33cm \div 2.5cm = 13"$
Example 2: $2.5m \div 0.9m = 3 \text{ yds.}$

For seam allowances, you can use whatever you like—1/2", 5/8". Sewing a costume does not require the same precision as sewing garments.

Glossary of British Terms

* buckram—*a stiff linen cloth*
  colored PVC or fablon—*Contact® paper*
  copydex—*similar to rubber cement*
  elastoplast—*stretchable band-aid*
* kapok—*loose batting (use Polyfil or equivalent)*
* lurex—*metallic stretch fabric*
* marquisette—*a crisp, sheer fabric*
* petersham—*thick corded silk ribbon*
* plasticine—*Play Doh or malleable clay*
  polythene sheet—*acetate or see-through plastic*
  pop socks—*knee socks*
* press stud—*gripper snap*
  sellotape—*Scotch® tape*
* shirring elastic—*elastic thread for bobbin*
* stanley knife—*X-acto knife*
* vilene—*non-woven interfacing*
* voile—*sheer, semicrisp fabric*
* wadding—*cotton or polyester batting*
* wincyette—*inexpensive lining fabric*

* *available in fabric or craft stores*

Acknowledgements

As with most things I seem to take on, this book had to be produced in an enormous rush to meet the publisher's deadline, and I could never have made it without help from a wonderful team that I managed to get together. Also, although I knew exactly how I wanted a costume to look, very often I was unsure as to how to achieve it, and I was lucky enough to be able to use the professional skills of some designer friends. Vin Burnham, who makes wonderful costumes for films, opera and so on, made for me the beautiful butterfly, the Humpty Dumpty, the firework headdress and the postcard Samurai. Her sister Lal D'Abo sewed the clown, the ghost, the little witch, Red Riding Hood, the ballerina and the small butterfly. David Blight constructed for me the galleon, the pillar, St George, the dictionary and showed me how to make the strong papier-mâché head shapes. Sally Turner did marvellous work on some of the 'through the ages' costumes, Jan Blake put together the Victorian couple, the knickerbockerglory, the can-can dancer and Jekyll and Hyde, and Charlotte Humpston battled away to sew the Pair of the Same Suit and the Gemini outfits.

For the rest of the costumes I owe an enormous debt to Jill Thraves. Without her help and brilliant talent as a seamstress I would never have been able to produce half of them in time. Jill came to my house every day, and from my sketches would cut out and sew a finished costume. She put up with children running in and out, dogs, telephone calls, family crises and all the other paraphernalia of daily life, and calmly continued to help

me produce our creations. When the book was finished I think we both missed our little workshop, and I am grateful to her not only for helping me to produce the book, but also for the fun we had in working together.

As with my book on party cakes[1] which I wrote last year, I must thank Bryan Wharton for his beautiful photographs. He moved smoothly from photographing tiny details on iced cakes to accommodating large costumes of every kind. He more or less had to abandon his studio totally to this project for a few weeks, and I am very grateful for his hard work, support and encouragement.

I have another cake book ex-worker to thank – my mother. As with that project, she again patiently put up with my untidiness and kept careful lists of which costumes were finished, what accessories would be needed when they were photographed, and so on, as well as laboriously packing up and putting away those that were completed. Thank you too to Mike Norriss and Flora Casement for their practical help.

My husband helped me enormously with ideas, and to him and my daughter Katie many thanks not only for their help, but also for putting up with the chaos that the making of the book inevitably produced in the house.

Finally I must thank all of my beautiful models, who so patiently wore some extraordinary outfits with great cheerfulness and cooperation. I hope they got as much fun out of the sessions as I did.

1. *Jane Asher's Party Cakes* (Pelham Books)

Introduction

Trying on mummy's things.

It's never too young to start.

'By the way Mum, I need to be the Archangel Gabriel by 9.0 tomorrow morning for the school play.' This sort of challenging statement thrown casually over the shoulder by a nine year old engrossed in 'Top of the Pops' or whatever may be familiar to many parents. I certainly remember making such demands myself as a child.

We always had a dressing-up cupboard at home, where my mother and father hoarded all the old clothes, shoes and hats they no longer wore, as well as things found at jumble sales and so on. From an early age my brother, sister and I enjoyed parading around in strange assortments of pieces of clothing, not necessarily corresponding in any rational way to the character we were imagining ourselves to be. There seems to be an instinct in all children to dress up; I certainly notice in my own son and daughter the early desires to be disguised and to pretend to be

somebody or something else, and the feelings all children have to want to be more grown up than they are being expressed first of all in a trying on of Mummy's things.

In many people these instincts seem to stay with us into adulthood; I am lucky enough to be in a profession where I can indulge them to the full. I still get a thrill when I am decked out in some beautiful period costume – in spite of some of them being extremely uncomfortable. This points out, of course, one of the great advantages of fancy dress as compared to dressing professionally for film or stage: when dressing purely for fun you can make your costume as comfortable as you like, and have no worries at all about being historically accurate. For an Elizabethan costume, for instance, you can use without any qualms a fabric that wasn't invented until three hundred years later, or make a very pleasing stone-age bikini from nylon fake fur! Fun and effect and low price are the only criteria.

People have been wearing fancy dress for many many years – one of the earliest forms of course was simply to paint the body with patterns, usually having some ceremonial or religious significance. Costumes and masks took over from paint for dressing up purposes as man began to wear clothes, and by the time of the Borgias the masked ball had become an extremely popular form of entertainment. Rome and Venice were the centres for these masques, and their popularity soon spread across Europe, and by the seventeenth century they were a regular feature of court life in England. The architect Inigo Jones was much involved in the masques and designed magnificent costumes and elaborate scenery. One of the attractions seems to have been the change of character and relaxing of morals that was possible once a disguise was assumed. At the Roman carnival held every year maskers were even protected by the guards and

A costume of Grimaldi, the famous clown, made in the 1880s for my Grandfather.

given free rein to insult and imitate figures of dignity such as priests and lawyers.

The maskers went to extraordinary lengths to produce unusual costumes; the landscape painter Sam Bough went to a party as the devil with a tail containing a live eel which writhed and coiled until four in the morning. The poor creature was revived from time to time by Bough's sitting on the edge of a fountain with his 'tail' in the water.

The Victorians considered fancy dress balls an essential part of society life; for Queen Victoria's Jubilee a ball was held at the Mansion House which began with 150 children representing the sovereigns since the Conquest and their most notable subjects. The star part of Queen Elizabeth I was played by a nine year old. I doubt if her costume was made of glue and pasta as is our nine year old Elizabeth (p. 33).

In more recent years the most famous fancy dress occasion has been the Chelsea Arts Ball which, apart from the War, was held every year until 1958,

Costumes made in 1913 for the Chelsea Arts Ball . . . and still going strong today.

Well now there is no need to hire a dressmaker! Here are over one hundred costumes for you to make at home. I have tried to keep the materials as inexpensive as possible, often using old curtains, lavatory paper, cardboard boxes and so on. There are various alternative ways given of making things, so that you can swop materials and methods for any of the costumes to suit your own requirements. There are also some quick ideas involving very little dressing up, for those who prefer the more subtle approach, and who want to be able to go to the party without looking like a Christmas Tree (talking of which, see p. 127). The cutting out patterns are drawn on squared paper, so that I think you will be able to scale them up and down to whatever size you need — I have given the age of the child or size of the adult for whom each one was made, to help you to work out the necessary measurements. And obviously all the costumes are interchangeable from child to adult and vice-versa.

I do hope these costumes will be a springboard for your own ideas: the possibilities are limitless once you get going. I have incorporated a lot of theatrical tricks for making an effect cheaply and quickly and on the addresses page (p. 141) you will find some shops much patronised by theatre and film designers that you may not have discovered before. I hope you have enormous fun making them, and incorporating some of the ideas and methods in your own designs.

The photographic sessions were enormous fun for everyone . . .

. . . but very exhausting!

usually at the Royal Albert Hall. It was normally on New Year's Eve, and a fairly typical evening would involve at least 3500 guests, with people flying in from Hollywood and all over Europe. One year an artificial snowstorm was staged with six enormous sackfuls of fake snow poured down onto the dancers from the roof 130 feet (40m) above. Dressmakers were hired to make the most elaborate costumes and enormous decorated floats formed the centrepiece on the dance floor.

Britannia

This dress was originally made by my mother in beautiful parachute silk for me to go to a party in many years ago. It has survived intact and been worn by many children since, only needing slight re-furbishing and, recently, a new helmet and shield.

MATERIALS

(To fit 8–10 year old)
1.15m white silky looking fabric, 90cm or 115cm wide
shirring elastic
red, white and blue ribbon, or some of each
cardboard
red, white and blue crêpe paper
Union Jack (or use the crêpe paper)
long stick
silver foil
spray glue
tape

Cut 2 shapes from card as fig. 1, and cover outsides with spray glue and silver foil. Cut 5cm wide strips of crêpe paper in all three colours and placing them on top of each other gather them slightly into a frill and tape them to the inside of one helmet half as shown. Place the other half on top and staple them together, sandwiching the frill in between. Staple ribbons to tie under chin.

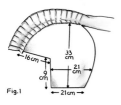

Fig.1

Join the piece of fabric into a tube, using the width of the fabric as your length of dress. With shirring elastic in the bobbin of your machine, stitch four rows at waist and top to gather gently. Add ribbon shoulder straps.

Cut a shield shape from cardboard and cover with either a real Union Jack or make one by sticking strips of crêpe paper onto it. Fix a handle at the back by sticking and taping a strip of card.

Cut trident shape from card, cover with silver foil and tape to top of long stick.

Firework (or Hayley's Comet)

I have known and admired Hayley Mills since we were both child actresses – after starring in 'Tiger Bay' and 'Pollyanna' she was the one that all of us others looked up to. Now she has a whole new generation of admirers of my daughter's age, since her delightful performance in 'The Flame Trees of Thika'. I don't think her temperament is as explosive as this costume, but her personality is certainly as bright and sparkly.

MATERIALS

(To fit adult)
For base
length of corrugated cardboard about 1m long and 1.2 m wide, with joins if necessary
2.5m crinoline hoop 1cm wide
webbing
extra cardboard for 'flash' on base
green, red and yellow spray paints
1 packet blue crêpe paper
strong tape
glue

For headdress
about 30 lengths of cane each approx. 85cm long, taken from cane blind
different coloured chiffon or net
gathered or pleated gold and silver tissue
Uhu glue
tight fitting old hat or hat base
foam rubber
Evostick
glitter

BASE

Cut length of cardboard long enough to fit around body. Spray it green and glue on lightning shape cut from cardboard and sprayed red. Spray yellow around shape. Attach crinoline hoop and webbing straps as for Christmas Cracker (p. 131).

Cut 1.10m length of crêpe paper. Glue the long edge along inside top edge of cardboard. Fit the cardboard shape on the wearer, staple and tape edges together at the back and gathering crêpe around neck, tie blue wool or cord around neck.

HEADDRESS

Make a hat base from a fairly solid old hat – preferably something like a bowler with the brim cut off. Make it fit as snugly as possible, sticking little bits of foam inside if necessary to wedge it (fig. 1).

Fig. 1

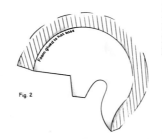

Fig. 2

Glue a strip of foam rubber 8cm thick and about 10cm wide down centre of hat shape from front to nape. Use Evostick and make sure it sticks very firmly (fig. 2).

Make flames by cutting strips of coloured chiffon as fig 3.

Run a line of Uhu down each cane and stick to centre of chiffon strip, leaving about 8cm of cane protruding to stick into foam. Decorate with a little spray glue and glitter dust.

Put Uhu onto ends of flames and stick into foam rubber, getting someone else to hold the base.

Gather or pleat metallic material or paper and cut spiky ends (fig. 4).

Stick or sew all round base of hat, hiding the foam. Keep trying on for balance, adding more foam inside if necessary to help it not to slip.

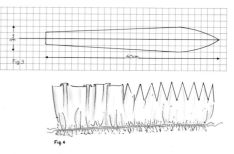

Fig. 3

Fig. 4

Pixie on Toadstool

I love these *trompe-l'œil* effects – this worked so effectively that Bryan Wharton, our photographer, thought Millie really was sitting on the toadstool, and got quite a shock when it walked into position.

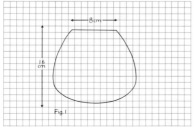

MATERIALS

(To fit 8–10 year old)
20cm yellow felt, 90cm wide
20cm purple felt, 90cm wide
50cm green felt, 90cm wide
1.3m thick wadding
60cm petersham or webbing for waistband
5.6m rigilene or corrugated cardboard
60cm pink felt, 90cm wide
scraps of red material

PIXIE

Cut 3 shapes in yellow and 3 in purple (fig. 1).

Alternating colours and overlapping the pieces, stitch together to form collar (fig. 2).

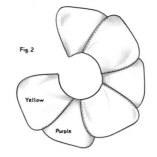

Join ends at back with hook and eye.

Cut 3 shapes in yellow and 3 in purple (fig. 3).

Stitch together in same way as collar to form little skirt.

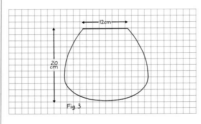

Cut 2 leg shapes in pink (fig. 4).

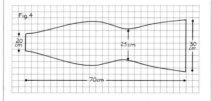

Fold lengthwise, stitch down back seam and turn right side out. Stuff lightly with a little wadding and tack together at tops.

Cut 4 pieces of green felt (fig. 5).

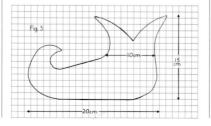

Place the 4 pieces in pairs and stitch around outer edge, leaving ankle open. Place bottom of each leg in a boot and tack to hold.

Cut 2 shapes in green felt (fig. 6).

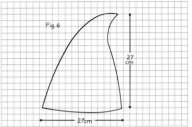

Stitch together around outside edge, leaving bottom open.

TOADSTOOL

Make 2 circles of rigilene, one 1.2m circumference, one 2m circumference by stapling ends together. Add spokes about 30cm long, bending ends over outside circle and stapling, taping to inner circle and bending over petersham strip at centre for waistband and stapling (fig. 7). Stitch hook and eye onto waistband. Alternatively make in similar way as for Tortoise Shell (p. 92), but round and with hole and split it for getting in and out.

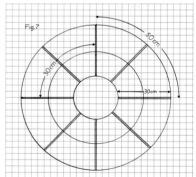

Cover shape with the wadding, tacking edge underneath outside circle.

Glue circles of red fabric onto wadding.

Cut strip of remaining wadding to fit around real legs. Wrap around and tack edges together and tack top to underneath of toadstool.

Ballerina

I know my stepdaughter Araminta would far rather be dancing at a disco party than at the ballet, but she can't help looking very beautiful in this simple but romantic outfit.

MATERIALS

(to fit size 10–12)
about 80cm of wide belt elastic
15.3m white net 150 cm wide
1.2m white elastic
silver and pearlised sequins
glue
white leotard

Cut 3 lengths of net: 6m for top layer, 5m for middle layer and 4m for under layer. Keeping it double, fold each length into about 8 thicknesses and cut V shapes out of hem. Attach to elastic as for good and bad fairies (p. 120), ignoring the top layer of decorated net and instead gluing a few sequins at random on the net.

Cut 3 more strips of net 10cm wide with jagged edges like the skirt and gather onto 2 lengths of elastic to fit the upper arms and onto a length to go around head. Join ends into circlets. Wear skirt over leotard.

VALENTINE'S DAY Heart

I think Tanya looks delicious in this, and would cause many other hearts at a party to be pierced. What you wear round the back is up to you . . . If you were going as a couple, then Cupid would make a good companion — just a short version of the Greek boy (p. 27), plus a cardboard bow and arrow covered in silver foil.

MATERIALS

(To fit adult)
1m red 'satin' lining 115cm wide
1m medium weight wadding
cardboard
6m trimming lace, or old net curtain
    cut up
four pieces of tape for tying

Cut one shape in card, one in wadding and one in red fabric as fig. 1.

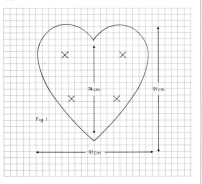

Fig. 1

74 cm 91 cm 91 cm

Sew wadding to red fabric around edge then gather lace into a frill round the outside. Staple or stick heart to card shape and attach tapes to fit comfortably over shoulders, crossing at back. Spray garden cane silver, add paper flights and pierce heart! Add silver foil tip.

Peter Carrot

It was the colour of my brother Peter's hair that inspired this carrot costume – and probably a subconscious tie-up in my mind with Peter Rabbit, who seemed to eat a good many of them. As children we frequently used to be called 'carrots' or 'copper nobs', and sometimes even the 'Carrots of Wimpole Street' – which was where we lived. That was quite funny the first dozen or so times . . .

MATERIALS

(To fit adult)
3m orange cotton fabric 115cm wide
3m lining fabric 115cm wide
6m medium weight wadding
2m 10cm crinoline hoop (inc. overlap) 1.5cm wide
2m tape 2.5cm wide
1m green cotton fabric (or crêpe paper) 90cm wide
7.3m plastic covered gardening wire
kitchen funnel
narrow elastic
glue

BODY

Cut two shapes in lining and two in wadding as fig. 1.

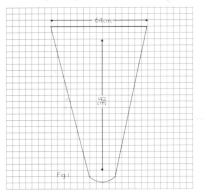

Pin wadding to inside of each lining shape and stitch around edge. Cut long strips of wadding 5–10cm wide and place horizontally at intervals on the wadding side of the carrot shapes. These will produce the bumpy look of the finished carrot. Tack in place (fig. 2).

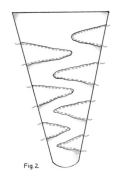

Fig 2

Working downwards from the top of each half, pin cotton fabric over wadding, making generous allowance for the raised strips. Trim cotton around edges. Machine cotton, through wadding, to lining around edges and on either side of wadding strips.

Right sides together, stitch carrot halves together, leaving top edge open. Stitch tape 2.5cm down from top edge to form channel for hoop, leaving 5cm open for threading and joining.

Cut three circles as fig. 3, one cotton, one lining, one wadding making hole in centres for head and slit at back centre for stepping in.

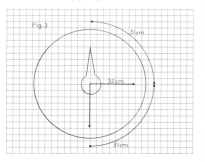

Fig 3

Stitch wadding between lining and cotton pieces. Gather circumference of circle into top edge of carrot, right sides together, matching centre fronts, back and sides.

Cut holes for arms approx. 50cm around just below crinoline hoop on each side. Cut leg holes approx. 75cm below arm holes and 60cm around. Finish off raw edges by binding and hemming. Fasten neck edge with hook and eye (fig. 4).

Fig 4

HEADDRESS

Cut eight strips each 11cm across of green fabric (or crêpe paper). Fold in two, end to end, and stitch a narrow channel down centre for wire. Cut 8 lengths of wire each about 90cm long, fold in two and twist together. Thread doubled wires into channels then slash the fabric on either side of the wire (fig. 5).

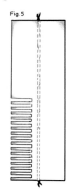

Fig 5

Twist these fronds together at base, push through funnel and tape on inside if necessary. Cover base with more shredded fabric and glue in place. Attach narrow elastic through holes punched in funnel.

Harlequin

Cut two pieces for front and back, and two sleeves (fig. 1).

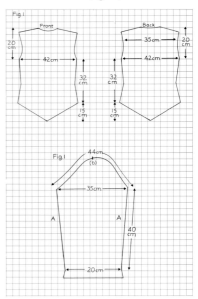

Right sides together, sew front and back at shoulders and side seams. Cut 15cm slit at back of neck.

Fold sleeves right sides together and stitch along underarm seams in both.

Right sides together, matching sleeve seams to side seams of body and marks 'b' to shoulder seams, pin and stitch sleeves into armholes, easing where necessary.

TROUSERS

Cut two pieces as fig. 2.

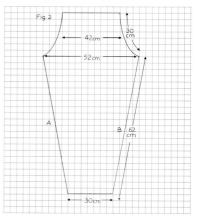

This fabric comes in many lovely bright colours and is very effective. Faye wears it beautifully, but of course it would equally well suit a boy, and you could make a Columbine to go with him – (see Ballerina, p. 16 plus a few paper flowers).

MATERIALS

(To fit 10–12 year old)
2.2m diamond patterned fabric 91cm wide
20cm white buckram
60cm elastic for waist
30cm narrow elastic for hat mask

Jester

Fold each piece right sides together bringing edges A to edges B. Stitch along this edge, forming legs. Turn right sides out. Right sides together, matching inside leg seams, stitch seam between legs marked C (fig. 3).

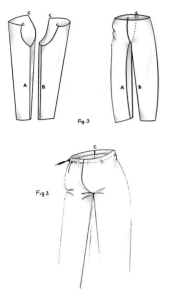

Fig. 3

Fig 3

Turn inside 25mm at waist edge and stitch to form channel for elastic, leaving small opening for threading.

HAT

Cut two shapes in buckram as fig. 4.

Stitch together along top edge. Attach narrow elastic to fit under chin where marked on fig. 4.

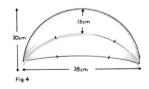

13cm

20cm

38cm

Fig. 4

A jester in the old days was employed by the king to bring some humour to the court – I imagine the modern equivalent in Buckingham Palace is to switch on the television. Here is a jolly jester to brighten up any party – and would go very well with a King Lear for a couple.

MATERIALS

*jerkin made as for Robin Hood
(p. 107), but in half yellow and half
red cotton*

For hat
50cm red cotton 115cm wide
50cm yellow cotton 115cm wide
2 bells
wadding
press stud

Cut 2 red and 2 yellow as shown in
fig. 1.

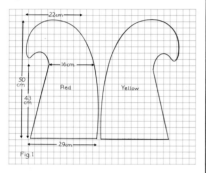

Fig 1

In one red and one yellow cut out
half face hole as fig. 2.

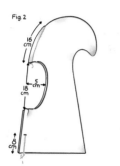

Fig 2

Place red and yellow fronts right sides
together and stitch up as shown in
fig. 2. Stitch centre back seam. Right
sides together, join front to back
around outside edge, leaving bottom
straight edge open. Hem face
opening. Add press stud under chin.
Turn right side out, stuff 2 horns with
wadding, tacking to side seams to
hold if necessary. Stitch bells to tips
of horns.

Wear with red or yellow polo neck
and tights, and jerkin.

Palm Tree

Another beautiful tree worn by
my friend Therese Sorrell (see
Christmas Tree) – this one was
her idea. I think the draped fabric
looks very attractive and could be
worn as an unusual evening dress
afterwards without the headdress.

MATERIALS

(To fit tall adult, size 10)
3.5m beige fabric 170cm wide
1 packet green crêpe paper
4m rigilene
*1 strip of buckram 61cm long ×
51mm wide*

Using complete piece of beige fabric
from one end mark with pins or chalk
at edges six 26cm widths. Starting at
other end mark off six 31cm widths
(fig. 1).

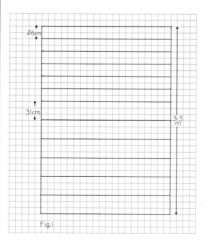

Fig.1

With wider markings nearest you,
bring lower edge of fabric up to meet
upper edge and pin together along
marked lines, forming folds (fig. 2).
You now have a 'lining' with folds on
top.

Right sides together stitch back seam,
forming tube. Stitch across top at
shoulders, leaving opening for head.
Cut armholes at sides.

Cut six varied lengths of rigilene
50–80cm long and six matching
lengths of green crêpe paper 20cm
wide. Sew rigilene down centre of
each paper strip and fringe edges.
Make headband of buckram and
stitch leaves around it. Wrap a further
strip of green paper 20cm wide
around headband and fringe edges.
Stitch circle of rigilene to insides of
leaves 10cm above headband.

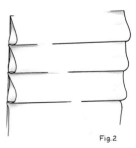

Fig.2

Red Indian

A very traditional costume, and one that I think boys still like to wear. This headdress uses feathers from a feather duster, which is a much cheaper way of buying them than individually, and means you get some lovely bright colours. I hope Sam doesn't have to run from any cowboys – from the look of his trousers he wouldn't get very far!

MATERIALS

(To fit 4–6 year old)
strip of leather look fabric
feathers from feather duster
stapler
pasta wheels
beads
spray paint

For tunic and trousers see Father Christmas (p. 128), but made in brown fabric, sewn up centre front with V cut at neck, and decorated with appliqué designs if wished.

Staple feathers all along leather strip, and decorate by gluing on pasta wheels, painted different colours. Add thin strips of leather to hang down, adding feathers, beads etc. Spray ends of feathers as wished.

Shorter Oxford Dictionary

A bit difficult to look up a word in this dictionary – probably easier to look down. But Martha looks so very sweet that she would be far more attractive on your shelf than the real thing.

MATERIALS

(To fit 2–4 year old)
corrugated cardboard
blue, white and gold paint
gold coloured wood glue (p. 140)
stapler

Cut two shapes from corrugated cardboard as fig. 1.

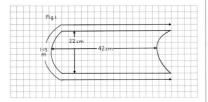

Cut a hole in top piece 56cm circumference, remembering you will use it with ridges upwards, to resemble pages. Cut a larger more oblong hole in the other piece for the legs. Bend the curved edges all round up into tabs, by slitting (fig. 2).

Cut a piece of corrugated cardboard 1.15m by 60cm and bend into book shape, then staple to tabs of 'pages' as fig. 3. Add a further piece to fit at the front. Make sure ridges of this piece go downwards.

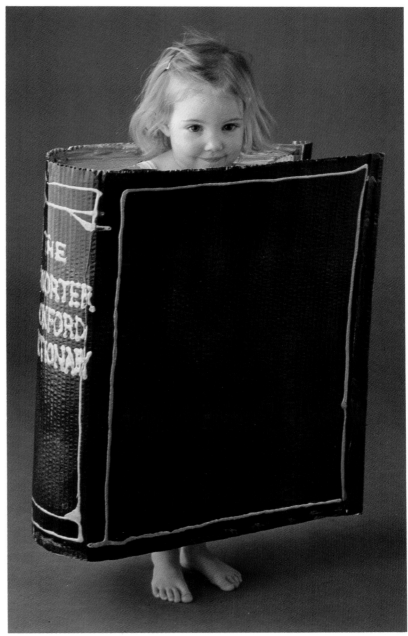

Paint 'pages' gold on the top and white at the side. Paint cover blue, and when dry decorate with the wood glue. Make holes for arms if desired. Slide into book from below.

THROUGH THE AGES

I thought it would be fun to take a young couple through the ages in costume. I have used many different methods and materials, most of which are interchangeable, and they would all be equally suitable for adults, so I hope they will be useful as the basis for many different period outfits.

All these costumes were made to fit a boy of 10 and a girl of 9.

Stone Age

It seemed very boring to make brown fur costumes for the stone age, so I decided to make them in interesting colours. They're obviously made from the skins of some prehistoric creatures that have since become extinct — dyed-out I suppose.

BOY

MATERIALS

1m fake fur fabric 90cm wide
spray paint
30cm felt for thonging

Spray fur first in circles or stripes. When dry fold fabric and cut 2 shapes very roughly as fig. 1.

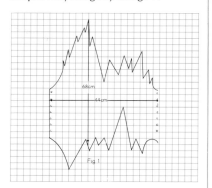

68cm
44cm
Fig. 1

Makes holes at sides and join together by thonging, either with long strips of felt, or with ribbon or string.

GIRL

MATERIALS

1m fake fur 90cm wide
spray paint
30cm felt for thonging
Das
scrap red felt for claws

First spray fur fabric in spots or stripes, etc.

When dry cut out two shapes as fig. 1. Add felt claws to paw.

Join together by cutting holes in sides and thonging with strips of felt or ribbon or string.

For top cut out 2 shapes as fig. 2.

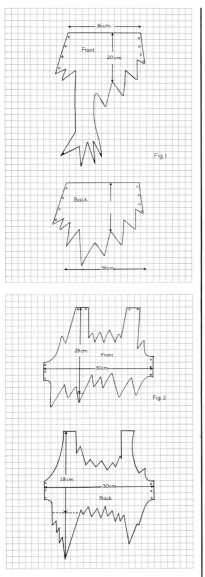

Fig. 1

Fig. 2

Thong together side and shoulder seams.

Make 'stone' necklace by moulding stones with holes in from Das. Spray, then thread with thonging.

Greek

These sort of costumes are so wonderfully easy to make – just lengths of fabric draped attractively in position. Most of us at one time or another have wandered around the bathroom wearing a couple of towels, delivering a brilliant speech to the assembled Grecian multitudes – you can throw them into almost any position and they look fairly authentic.

BOY

MATERIALS

1m white polyester jersey 170cm wide
1m yellow polyester jersey 170cm wide
brooch
gold foil and gold parcel ribbon
gold belt and sandals

Cut white fabric in half lengthwise, and tie top corners of one half to top corners of the other half to form a

Medieval

tabard. Cut yellow fabric in half lengthwise and stitch the two pieces end to end to make a piece 3m long.

Wear white tabard with knots on shoulders and pouched over belt. Wear yellow piece draped diagonally across body, passing under left arm with seam at side, and joining over right shoulder with brooch.

Cut gold ribbon to tie around head, and staple on leaf shapes cut from gold foil.

GIRL

MATERIALS
1.3m white polyester jersey 170cm
wide
gold braid
sandals
shirring elastic

Cut 1.1m of white fabric in half lengthwise, place one piece on top of other and cut scalloped shapes out of top edge. Tack both pieces together at points of scallop shapes, forming long tabard. Cut 85cm off remaining 20cm width, and with shirring elastic in bobbin of machine, stitch 4 close rows along one edge to gather up. Fasten with hook and eye.

Wear peplum over tabard, pouching top slightly. Wind gold braid around hair.

Both these outfits are made from very wide, inexpensive polyester, which comes in some lovely colours. I happened to find a belt that matched in an Oxfam shop, but a gold one would also look fine.

GIRL

MATERIALS
1m buckram
2.5m medium weight wadding
gold braid
1m chiffon or a remnant 90cm wide
3m turquoise fabric, 152cm wide
black dylon fabric paint
belt

Make buckram into a cone, making the widest end large enough to fit around head. Glue and staple together. Cut a strip 5cm wide of wadding and decorate with dashes of fabric paint to resemble ermine. When dry stick to edge of hat.

Cut 1 front and 1 back from turquoise fabric as figs 1 and 2.

Sew together at shoulder and side seams, leaving a 25cm gap for arms and neck. Make tucks on shoulder seams as for medieval boy.

Cut away at neck front as shown in fig. 1.

Add trimming to neck line by twisting a strip of material with some gold braid. Add 5cm strip of 'ermine' (see hat) around neckline, overlapping at front to form 'V' shape (see fig. 1).

Cut 2 sleeves as fig. 3 in dress fabric, cut 2 more in wadding but 5cm wider to make turned back cuffs (see dotted line in fig. 3).

Decorate wadding to resemble ermine (see hat).

When 'ermine' is dry, place a fabric shape on top of each wadding shape with wrong sides together and turn the extra 5cm of wadding over the fabric edge and stitch.

Fold sleeves as shown in fig. 4, right sides together, and stitch underarm seams.

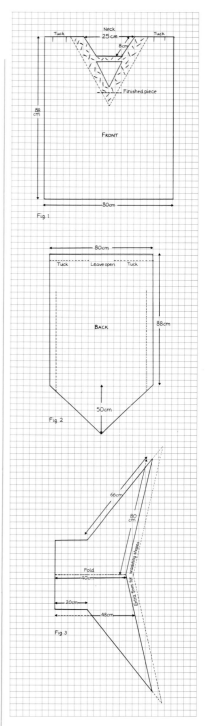

Turn right sides out and with right sides together, stitch into arm holes.

Make an 'ermine' strip 5cm wide and approx. 2.5m long and stitch around hem of dress.

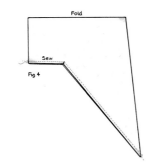

Fig. 4

Add a belt worn under the bustline if desired.

BOY

MATERIALS

2.1m brown polyester, 152cm wide
2.5m red felt, 90cm wide
remnants for hat, approx. 50cm
 square
old newspapers, tights etc for stuffing

TO MAKE HAT

Stuff one leg of a pair of tights (or one stocking) with newspaper. Stuff to right length to fit around head. Pull open end over foot end to make circle. Stitch. Cut fabric remnants into strips 8cm wide and sew end to end to make one long strip. Wind around stuffed shape to cover, stitching where necessary to hold it (fig. 1).

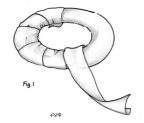

Fig. 1

Cut two pieces of brown polyester each 30cm by 152cm. Sew together end to end to form long strip. Cut one side into scallopped shape and attach end to side of hat. Add tassel to other end (fig. 2).

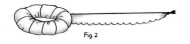

Fig. 2

To make the tassel cut a circle of polyester 15cm diameter, cut 10cm slashes around the outside then place a stone in the middle and tie tightly with cotton or wool (fig. 3).

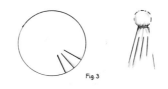

Fig. 3

CAPE

Cut two pieces as fig. 4 from felt. Right sides together sew along dotted lines, clipping corners as shown. Turn to right side.

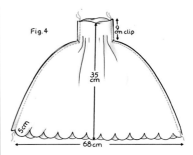

Fig. 4

TUNIC

Cut two rectangles each 75cm by 80cm in polyester. Sew together along dotted lines, leaving openings for neck and armholes as shown (fig. 5).

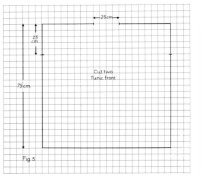

Fig.5

Cut two
Tunic front

25cm
25cm
75cm

Make two 5cm tucks on each shoulder seam.

For sleeves cut two as fig. 6. Fold as shown and stitch under arm seam.

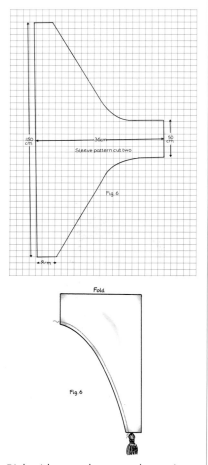

150cm   36cm   50cm
Sleeve pattern cut two
8cm
Fig. 6

Fold

Fig. 6

Right sides together, sew sleeves into armholes. Add a tassel to end of each sleeve, made as before (fig. 7).

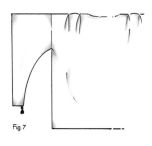

Fig.7

MONEY BAG

Cut a circle of fabric or felt 30cm in diameter. Make small holes around edge and thread string in and out. Pull tight and add plaited strips of felt to attach to belt. For shoes cut two shapes in felt as fig. 8. Fold and stitch as shown. Turn to right side and sew long toe point to front of shoe, adding tassel made as before but with ball of newspaper instead of stone so that it is light.

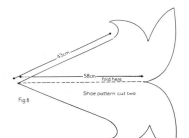

43cm   58cm fold here
Shoe pattern cut two
Fig. 8

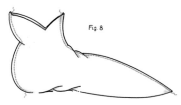

Fig. 8

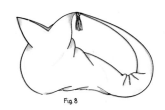

Fig. 8

Henry VIII

I've tried to vary the materials used in these 'Through the Ages' costumes, and this Henry is made almost entirely of felt. You could use many other fabrics of course, but one of the great advantages of felt, especially in a costume with lots of separate strips like this one, is that it doesn't fray and needs no finishing off at all.

MATERIALS

3.5m bright blue felt 90cm wide
2.1m pale blue felt 90cm wide
2.3m red velvet 90cm wide (or old velvet curtain)
pasta circles painted gold, silver and jewel colours
gold braid, chains, and pearls
remnant of thin white cotton, voile etc
cotton wool or wadding
red satin remnant
blue feather
elastic
newspaper, old tights etc for stuffing

Cut 4 shapes as fig. 1 in pale blue felt.

Fig. 1   60cm   A
39cm
52cm
19cm
68cm   B

Right sides together, stitch the two side seams A–B. Cut sixteen 52cm lengths of bright blue felt 5.5cm wide, and pin onto the right side of each of the pale blue pieces, at equal intervals, then stitch along waist and bottom edges (fig. 2).

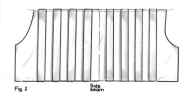

Fig. 2   Side seam

Right side in, join inside leg seam on each piece. Matching both these seams stitch crutch seam (fig. 3).

30

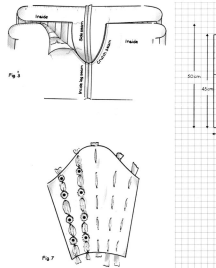

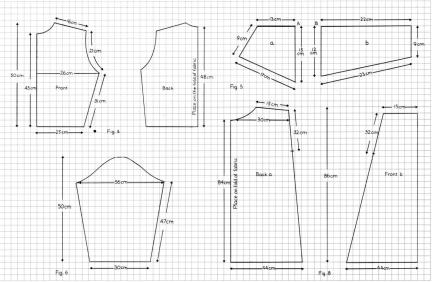

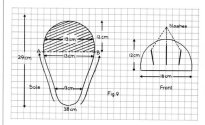

Turn to inside 2cm at waist and leg edges to form channel for elastic, leaving a gap for threading. Thread with elastic.

FOR JACKET

Cut 2 fronts and 1 back as fig. 4, in bright blue felt. Stitch fronts to back at shoulder and side seams.

FOR PEPLUM

Cut 2 shapes in bright blue as fig. 5a and 2 as fig. 5b. Gather the lower edge of each front into the top edge of 5a, with corners A at centre front waist. Stitch both pieces 5b onto lower edge of back, with corners B at centre back.

FOR SLEEVES

Cut 2 pieces of bright blue felt as fig. 6.

Make 5 vertical broken slashes in each piece, place a long strip of white thin fabric about 7cm wide behind each slash line and pull a little through each slit, tacking into place. Between each white puff glue a piece of the painted pasta (fig. 7).

Slash the jacket front in the same way and pull more white fabric through. Decorate front edges with pasta. Right sides inside, sew underarm seams in both sleeves, turn right sides out and, matching underarm seams to jacket side seams, and centre top

sleeves to shoulder seams, stitch both sleeves in.

FOR COLLAR

Cut a 27cm length of bright blue felt 4cm wide. Fit neck edge of jacket along one edge and stitch. Gather up 80cm strips of white 5cm wide and stitch behind cuff edges. Trim collar, cuffs, front edges and peplum with gold braid. Fasten with poppers.

FOR ARMBANDS

Cut two pieces of red velvet 68cm by 30cm. Make two vertical slashes about 12cm either side of centre and edge with 'ermine' (see Medieval Girl p. 28) and gold braid. Right sides together join each band at the short edges and elasticate top and bottom to fit over sleeves.

FOR CAPE

Cut 1 back and 2 fronts as fig. 8 in red velvet. Make pleats in back neck edge to reduce measurement to 20cm and machine in place. Right sides together, stitch fronts to back at shoulders and side seams as shown by dotted lines, leaving 32cm open for arms. Make pleats in each shoulder to reduce measurement to 9cm and stitch down. Finish edges.

FOR HAT

Cut two circles of bright blue felt 36cm diameter and stitch together

round the edges. Cut a hole 16cm diameter in the centre of one thickness. Turn hat right side out and decorate front with pasta, pearls and a feather.

FOR SHOES

Cut a right and a left sole in bright blue as fig. 9. Cut 2 front pieces in bright blue and 2 more in pale blue as fig. 9. Cut 3 slashes in bright blue as shown and pull bits of pale blue through the slits and tack in place. Right sides together stitch the fronts over the soles around edges. Turn out and cut 2 strips of fabric 38cm by 5cm and stitch to the backs of the soles and to the sides of the front pieces. Stick or tack ties on, and stuff toes with wadding.

Make garter from long strip of slashed felt, gathered top and bottom.

Cut sash from red satin remnant fringed both ends.

Wear with suitable tights, and stuff tummy and pumpkin pants with wadding, newspapers, old tights etc.

Queen Elizabeth I

This dress looks so magnificently elaborate that it's hard to believe it's made from old curtains, glue, fruit gums, pasta and paper doilies. I've used some glass jewels on the bodice and sleeves because I happened to have them, but you could just as well use more fruit gums or boiled sweets. The curtains, which I found in a secondhand shop had a lovely shiny reverse side, so I used them inside out for all of the dress. It's always worth looking at the wrong side of any fabric.

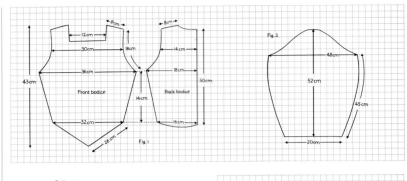

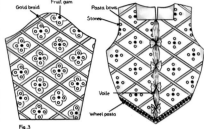

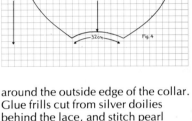

MATERIALS

2m white muslin or old net curtaining
2–3 curtains (or heavy fabric,
    brocade etc 115cm wide)
50cm stiff interfacing 90cm wide
3m rigilene
gold coloured wood glue (see p. 140)
white coloured wood glue (see p. 140)
fruit gums
pasta wheels sprayed gold and silver
pasta bows sprayed gold
glass stones
pearl drops and strings of pearls
white paper doilies
silver paper doilies
30cm open ended zip
40cm marquisette
gold remnant or gold braid
old lace curtain
60cm petersham for peplum, if not
    using curtains with rufflette
cardboard
millinery wire
stocking stuffed with newspaper
gold spray paint
vilene
shirring elastic

Cut as fig. 1, one front and two backs from curtain or fabric, and one front from interfacing. Stitch or iron interfacing to wrong side of front. Right sides together, stitch front to backs at shoulder and side seams. Hem lower edge of bodice. On wrong side, stitch a length of rigilene down centre front of bodice and along lower V-shaped edge. Finish off neck edge.

FOR SLEEVES

Cut 2 shapes as fig. 2. Using gold braid or strips of gold remnant, decorate sleeves and bodice in diagonal latticework. Stitch or glue in place. Pipe quatre-foil outlines in each space with gold glue, and decorate with white glue 'pearls' and fruit gum jewels in centres. Glue gold and silver wheel pasta along bottom edge and glue a glass stone or small boiled sweet in centre of each (fig. 3).

Tack a strip of white muslin or net down centre front, gather at intervals and glue gold painted bow pasta over.

Right sides in, stitch underarm seam in each sleeve and, matching underarm seam with side seam of bodice, and centre sleeve with shoulder seam, gather both sleeves into armholes.

Stitch white paper doily to end of each sleeve and turn back. Stitch zip down centre back as instructions on packet. For upright collar, cut piece of lace curtain and a piece of marquisette as fig. 4.

Stitch marquisette behind lace and add 30cm rigilene down centre dotted line. Spray lace gold. Cut 165cm of rigilene and pull out 3 of its plastic strands. Keeping them together, stitch with zig-zag all

around the outside edge of the collar. Glue frills cut from silver doilies behind the lace, and stitch pearl drops around the edge. Pin or stitch to back of bodice at shoulders after dress is put on.

LACE RUFF

Cut 7 white doilies in half and glue to a long strip of vilene 6cm deep. Fold into pleats and thread two rows of shirring elastic through, to tie around neck (fig. 5).

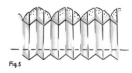

FOR SKIRT

Use one curtain (in this case the reverse side) about 1.5m wide and 1.02m deep. Spread on floor or table to decorate. With strips of white muslin/net about 7cm wide, make a lattice work pattern, tacking and gathering at each intersection, and gluing on a pasta bow. Add gold and 'jewelled' quatre-foils in each space, as for sleeves. When all is dry, right sides together stitch up back seam. Gather up the rufflettes to fit waist, or make channel and thread with elastic.

Victorian

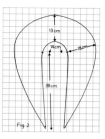

As with the Twenties Costume I didn't think it would be worth the effort of trying to tailor a jacket, but one couldn't have a Victorian man in his shirtsleeves, so I've compromised by having a fancy waistcoat and a cloak. I've cut down an old cloak of mine that I wore while pregnant which is why it is lined, but for dressing up purposes I have given instructions to make it without lining. And look what has happened to the Christmas Pudding (p. 130) — it makes a wonderful skirt.

LADY

MATERIALS

skirt as for Christmas Pudding (p. 130)
40cm same tweed or other fabric for bodice 115cm wide
1m tartan 115cm wide
1m cotton fabric for collar, peplum and bonnet 90cm wide
strip of lace remnant for bonnet frill
30cm velcro
card
copydex
stapler
full sleeved blouse

FOR BODICE

Cut 2 fronts and 1 back as fig. 1. Right sides in, stitch darts as shown. Cut triangle of tartan with 2 sides of 30cm and 1 side of 13cm. Turn and stitch narrow hem on the short side then place behind two fronts and stitch up one edge. On the other side stitch velcro to wrong side of bodice front, and to right side of tartan, to fasten across.
Right sides together, join fronts to back at shoulder and side seams.

FOR COLLAR

Cut 1 shape as fig. 2.
Stitch 2cm width tartan around inner and outer edges. Stich to bodice close to inner edge of collar, placing two points of collar at waist of bodice on either side (fig. 3).

FOR SKIRT

See Christmas Pudding (p. 130). Cut 9cm wide tartan strips for frill, then stitch onto bottom of skirt, gathering as you go.

FOR PEPLUM

Cut shape in brown cotton as fig. 4. Trim the edge with a 9cm frill as skirt. Gather straight edge to fit waist, and stitch to bodice at waist, matching A and B to centre fronts.

FOR BONNET

Cut 2 shapes in card and 2 in fabric as fig. 5. Glue fabric onto card, then staple straight edge AA to curved edge BB, fabric side out. Gather lace remnant into frill and glue to inside front. Cut 2 lengths of tartan, 35cm by 5cm gather each into rosettes and stitch to either side. Stitch a narrow 36cm length of tartan to each side for ties.

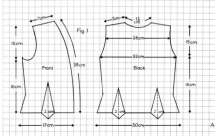

FOR PEPLUM

Either use an existing pelmet gathered up to fit waist, or ruffletted tops of two curtains, or cut enough fabric 20cm deep to make 3m length, joined if necessary, and gathered onto petersham to fit waist. Put on over skirt and add hook and eye at back or pin.

To support skirt, cut circle of thick card 53cm diameter, and an oval hole 23cm by 19cm in centre. Cut opening at back large enough to slide in sideways. Wear this on top of the tightly-stuffed stocking tied around waist to help support it.

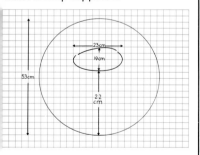

FOR HAIR

Thread pearls onto the millinery wire 75cm long and tape ends together. Bend into a heart shape and stitch pearl drop and glass stone to centre. Grip in place on top of backcombed hair.

Stitch 2 long pearl strings to each shoulder, adding jewel and pearl drop to centre of one. Wear pearl drop earrings.

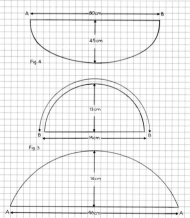

GENTLEMAN

MATERIALS

*2 old curtains or 2.5m of cream
    material 115cm wide
1 small curtain for waistcoat, or
    remnant about 1m by 90cm
brown felt tip pen
2m brown for cloak 115cm wide
2m black bias binding
scrap of lace for trimming
strong card
corrugated cardboard
black spray paint
black petersham, about 50cm
glue*

FOR TROUSERS

Cut 4 pieces from curtains or fabric as
fig. 1.

Make up as for Father Christmas (p.
128). Hem bottoms. Add brown
check with felt tip pen.

WAISTCOAT

Cut 1 back and 2 fronts as fig. 2.

Right sides together, stitch together at
shoulder and side seams. Trim edges
with black bias binding and decorate
with lace trimming. Add buttons, real
or painted on.

FOR CLOAK

Cut 2 shapes from brown fabric as fig.
3. Stitch together round neck edge
and finish off edges. Add fastening.

FOR HAT

Cut oval shape about 34cm long and
26cm across from strong card. Cut
away an oval shape from the middle
to fit on the head but allow for 2cm to
be turned up as shown (fig 4).

Cut a piece of corrugated cardboard
17cm by the exact crown
measurement. Butt ends together and
tape into a tube. Stick to brim, with
tabs on the inside. Cut another oval
piece of card to fit the top and stick.
Spray black and add a petersham
band when dry.

Fig.4   Tabs   Brim

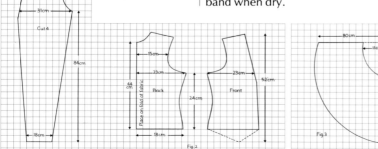

Twenties

The thought of tailoring a jacket was too daunting, but it wouldn't have been right for the immaculate look of the twenties for Jo to be in shirtsleeves, so his blazer is simply painted on to a sweat shirt. I think it looks very effective, and much more fun than wearing a real one.

BOY
MATERIALS

1 white sweat shirt, or long-sleeved T-shirt
dylon fabric paint, spray paint, and/or felt-tip pen
red crêpe paper
scraps for bow-tie
felt scraps for lapels
4 large coat buttons
silver foil
2m curtain lining or cotton 115cm wide
masking tape
60cm elastic
cardboard
white shirt

'JACKET'

Mark roughly where lapels are to go. Then mask off with tape stripes down the front and paint in between with fabric dye. Remove tape and fill in other stripes with felt-tip or different coloured dye.

Cut out lapels from felt and stick on with copydex. Draw in shirt details at neck with felt tip and draw shirt buttons. Cover coat buttons with silver foil and stitch onto 'jacket'.

To make carnation

Cut a strip of red crêpe paper 50cm long and 5cm wide, using pinking shears to cut one long side. Roll up and sellotape at base. Open up and sew onto lapel (fig. 1).

Bow tie

Fold a remnant 15cm square as fig. 2 and add a little strip in the middle, gathering it up to form a bow tie. Fix this to the top of the sweatshirt.

Wear a white shirt underneath the sweatshirt, letting only the collar and cuffs show.

FOR THE TROUSERS

Cut out 4 trouser pieces as fig. 3.

Right sides together, stitch outside and inside leg seams on each trouser leg. Turn 1 leg right side out and put this leg inside the other one. Stitch the crutch seam (fig. 4).

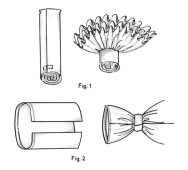

Fig. 1

Fig. 2

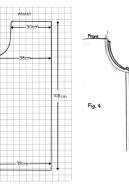

Fig. 3   waist   30cm   38cm   108cm   38cm

Fig. 4   Front   Back

Turn over small amount at top for channel for elastic and stitch, leaving opening for threading. Thread with elastic. Make turn-ups at bottom by turning and pressing 5cm twice, pressing creases at front and back of trousers and then tacking turn ups at side seams.

FOR THE HAT

Cut an oval shape out of card as fig. 5.

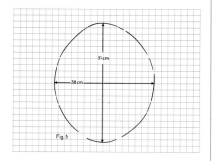

Fig.5

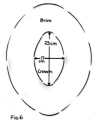

Fig.6

Cut an oval out of the centre as fig. 6, keeping cut out oval to become the crown. Cut a piece of corrugated cardboard 8cm by 66cm and sellotape this around the hole in the brim and around the crown, keeping the sellotape on the inside. Spray the hat and paint on a striped hat band.

GIRL

MATERIALS

3m fringing, 25cm deep
40cm lurex, 90cm wide
40cm lace curtaining, 90cm wide
40cm lining 90cm wide
1.20cm elastic, narrow
feathers and beads

Cut a rectangle 80cm by 34cm in both lurex and lace. Place the lace over the lurex and with right sides together stitch into a cylinder as fig. 1. This seam will go to the side.

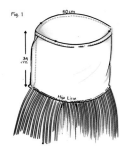

Fig. 1

Sew on fringe to lower edge, and hem the top edge. Sew a 10cm long piece of elastic to each side at top, to gather under the arms.

For shoulder straps, attach strong thread to front of bodice, about 12cm in from side seam, and thread with beads until it is 28cm long, then attach to back. Repeat for other side.

PETTICOAT

Cut a rectangle 80cm by 28cm from lining fabric. Right side in, stitch along short side to form cylinder. Hem both long sides, forming channel for elastic at top edge. Sew on fringing as fig. 2. Thread elastic through waist.

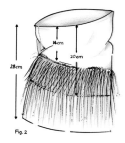

Fig.2

HEADDRESS

Cut a strip of lurex 54cm by 5cm. Right side in, fold it in half longways and stitch along the long side. Turn right side out and thread with 40cm of narrow elastic. Stitch into a circle through fabric and elastic. Decorate with feathers and beads.

Tie bows from ribbon or material onto party shoes.

Punk

There are some marvellous coloured hairsprays around now that can be easily washed out, but if you don't fancy using your own hair then these feathers make a very effective Mohican type hair-do. For the rest of the outfit you can really use your own imagination.

MATERIALS

feathers from feather dusters
cardboard
foam rubber
glue
black bin liner
safety pins
chains
remnants fabric, leopard skin, tartan

Cut two crescent shapes to fit over head from cardboard and one from foam rubber. Sandwich the foam between the cardboard and glue together. Glue feathers upright along either side. Grip to hair or stocking cap.
Construct clothes from the remaining materials, pinning together where necessary.

The Future

Who's to know what we shall be wearing in the future – but it's fun to concoct something imaginary. These two look as if they might even be a couple of robots: no doubt micro computers in the home will eventually be programmed to do almost anything we want, and perhaps they will be made to look more human than they do at present.

MATERIALS

bubble pack	*PVC tubing*
glue	*wire*
silver foil	*silver tights*
plastic beakers	*stapler*
sellotape	

Staple a balaclava shape from bubble pack (see p. 140), and staple plastic beakers all over it. Dress the wearers in bubble pack tubing, foil etc, allowing the imagination full rein.

Knickerbocker Glory

I think it's enormously to her credit that Joanna Lumley manages to be so funny in both her performing and writing while remaining so utterly glamorous and feminine. I have admired her for many years. She started her career as a model, and it was fascinating to watch her professionalism during our photo session. It is obviously a craft one doesn't forget; she slipped quickly into the 'glorious knickerbockers' and once the camera was focussed on her went into pose after pose – all beautiful and some balanced precariously on one high-heeled leg. It was impossible to decide which photograph to use, and who'd have thought anyone could look so good dressed only in lavatory paper and paper plates?

MATERIALS

(To fit size 10)
3.2m white material 115cm wide
1 roll each pink, green and white
*   lavatory paper*
small amount yellow lavatory paper
3 paper plates and one paper doily
scraps brown and red material
small amount green crêpe paper
elastic
copydex
brown crayon, red felt tip pen

Cut 2 backs and one front as fig. 1.

Make darts as fig. 1 and, right sides together, join side seams. Add elastic for shoulders, and hooks and eyes down back. Stitch white lavatory paper around top and over elastic, gathering into a frill as you go. Bunch up pieces of pink and green paper

and stick with copydex onto the front. Stick fruit (see below) among the bunches.

FOR KNICKERBOCKERS:

Cut 2 as fig. 2.

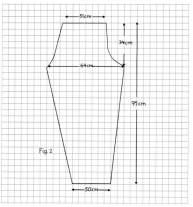

Onto these shapes sew frills of white, pink and green paper. In between frills stick strips of pink and green (fig. 3).

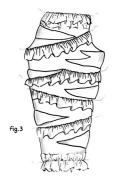

Place finished legs right sides together and sew crutch seams (fig. 4).

Open out the other way and sew inside leg seams (fig. 5).

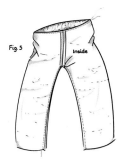

Turn under small amount at waist and ends of legs and stitch to form channels for elastic, leaving an opening for threading. Thread with elastic.

FOR HAT:

Stick two paper plates together in the middle, but with one placed crooked to the other (fig. 6).

Stuff bunched-up green paper in between one side of the plates to wedge them apart. Drape and stick with copydex several layers of white paper in a spiral shape onto the top plate, to create a whipped cream effect. Cut a wedge out of the third paper plate and cover with a piece of paper doily. Colour it brown with crayon and stick into the 'cream'.

TO MAKE THE FRUIT:

One piece of yellow paper folded into a wad and stuck together then cut into a strawberry or slice of peach shape. For strawberry, colour with red felt tip pen, leaving dots of yellow showing. Make leaves out of small pieces of green paper, and make chocolate sauce from strips of brown material.

Princess

Three or four years ago I saw a Princess dressing-up outfit in a chain store and thought how much my daughter would love it. I then looked at the price and was horrified, and decided I could make one even more glittery and rich looking at home if I put my mind to it. I bought a simple party dress pattern and adapted it slightly by opening up the front of the skirt and fitting a gold underskirt behind it. I made it from silky-looking lining material and some remnants of gold fabric, lace etc. The most extravagant buy was the jewels, which of course can always be taken off and used on something else, or you could decorate it with glue and fruit gums as with Queen Elizabeth (p. 33). The hat is a simple buckram shape covered with fabric and richly decorated.

Dragon

This outfit, although not easy, is not as complicated as it looks, and well worth a little effort. Again the beautiful fused nylon fabric comes into its own, although any bright green would do. It would be wonderful to have a flame thrower hidden inside, but one can carry enthusiasm a little too far . . .

MATERIALS

(To fit 8–10 year old)
3.5m green fabric 115cm wide
3.5m red lining 115cm wide
2m medium weight wadding
2 ping pong balls painted red
90cm velcro

Cut 1 front and two backs in green material, one front and two backs in wadding and one front and two backs in lining (fig. 1).

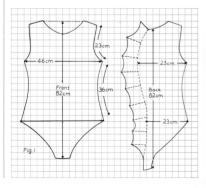

Sandwich wadding between fabric and lining and stitch around edges. On front stitch scale patterns through all three layers (fig. 2).

Place two back pieces on top of each other, linings together, and stitch together round outline of back fin, along 'spines' and down centre back seam, leaving small opening for tail (fig. 3).

Open out back and, right sides together, stitch to front at one shoulder seam, one side seam and between legs.

Cut two pieces in green fabric and 1 in wadding as fig. 4. Sandwich wadding between green pieces and sew around edge and along spine lines of fin (fig. 4). Insert tail into opening of back piece and stitch.

Fold remaining green fabric and lining in half and cut two wing shapes of each. Also cut two channel strips in green only (fig. 5).

Wrong sides together, join red lining to each green wing by stitching around edges. Stitch radiating spines. Stitch arm channel to top of each wing, A to A, leaving ends open (fig. 5).

Attach velcro to shoulder and side seams of body. Attach 10cm of velcro top and bottom of each wing on insides, and on either side of spine on body.

With materials still folded cut 2 of green, 2 of wadding and 2 of lining as fig. 6. Cut 4 ear shapes in green only.

Sandwich wadding between fabric and lining on both sides and stitch around edges. Pin darts as fig. 6 and stitch from edges in as far as indicated to leave eyeholes and nostrils.

Green sides out, stitch sides of head together from point A around edge to point B, matching darts. Stitch at base of fin and spines on fin (fig. 6).

Stick ping pong balls into eyeholes. Attach velcro at neck. Place ear pieces wrong sides together and stitch around edges. Fold each ear in half and attach to head.

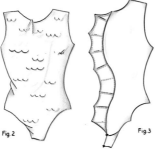

Fig. 2

Fig. 3

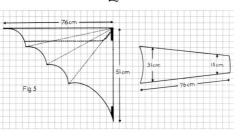

Fig. 4

18 cm

127cm

Fig. 5

76cm

51cm

31cm

15cm

76cm

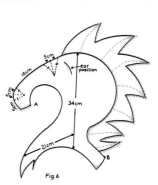

5cm

16cm

ear position

5cm

34cm

A

21cm

B

Fig. 6

St George

MATERIALS
(To fit adult)
corrugated cardboard
stapler
white paint
silver spray paint
white fabric
red fabric
cardboard
6 dishcloths sprayed silver
halo as for Angel Fish (p. 00)
6 paper plates
elastic
old gloves sprayed silver
millinery wire
silver foil
glue

Cut 2 shapes for sides and 1 shape for underneath as fig. 1.

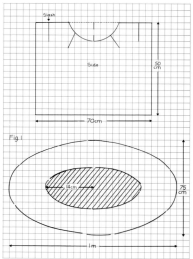

Fig.1

Slash tops of side pieces as shown. Overlap slightly where slashed and staple, making two rounded shapes. Slash and turn up tabs round edge of underneath and staple sides together and to tabs of base (fig. 2).

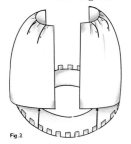

Fig.2

Christopher Cazenove has the sort of English good looks that set many a fair damsel's heart a-flutter, and who better to portray that symbol of Englishness and goodness than St George? It almost seems wicked to see him smoking (p. 103) after his dashing performance as our patron Saint. Mind you I'm not really sure I would want to be rescued by him – I should think any maiden in distress flung over this noble steed would cause the whole thing to collapse . . .

Cut 2 head shapes as fig. 3. Staple together with a long strip of corrugated cardboard in between, extending this strip at front and back for fixing to body (fig. 4). Paint all white, and add eye. Cut two more strips of corrugated cardboard for mane. Slash deeply and staple to either side of head. Add two cardboard ears. Staple head to body as firmly as possible – reins later will help to support it (fig. 5).

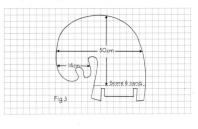

Fig. 3

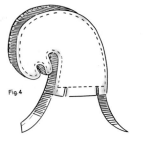

Fig. 4

Drape sides with white fabric to floor. Staple in place. Add a red saddlecloth on each side. Roll corrugated cardboard into tubes for legs. Curve two paper plates into cones for knee-caps, and bend two more as shown for feet. Staple onto legs (fig. 6).

Spray legs silver and staple to sides of horse.

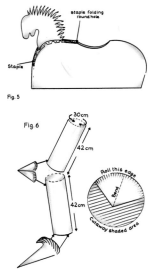

Fig. 5

Fig. 6

FOR HELMET

Cut 1 piece of corrugated cardboard for base and 2 pieces for visor as fig. 7. Bend on score line and overlap where slashed to form conical top. Tape two visor pieces together along lines A–B–C and stick to helmet above face hole. Paint all silver.

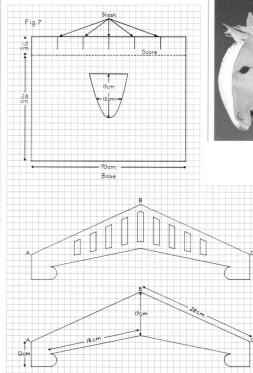

Fig. 7

Make hole in top of helmet. Twist pieces of millinery wire around strips of red fabric and insert into hole in top, splaying out wire underneath and taping to hold. Add a small strip of silver corrugated around the base of the wires just above helmet, for further support. Add a tail made like the mane.

Staple some strips of webbing at front and back of hole in top of horse to fit over the shoulders.

FOR CLOTHES

Pin silver dishcloths to arms and body (or sew together) for chain mail. Tack together two large squares of white fabric at shoulders to form tabard. Cut hole for neck. Add a red fabric cross to front.

Cut strips of red fabric for reins and staple to front of horse. For halo see Angel Fish (p. 101). Cut some cardboard into a sword shape and cover with silver foil.

If you wish to kill a dragon see p. 42.

Loch Ness Monster

I love to be in Soho when they celebrate the Chinese New Year — and one of the most splendid sights is the long winding Dragon that is supported on the heads of a long line of people. Well our monster doesn't quite match the magnificence of that creation, but the principle is the same, and it would be a marvellous way for a group of children to enter a party.

MATERIALS

(To be worn by 4 children)
cardboard box, about 50cm × 25cm
*   × 25cm*
Approx 12m bubble pack, 60cm
*   wide*
2 yoghurt cartons
French enamel varnish
2 pairs of bobbles on springs
*   removed from headbands*
stapler
paper

Cut away shaded areas from cardboard box as fig. 1.

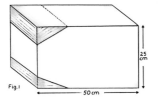

Fig.1   50cm   25cm

Score on dotted line and bring flap down to form head. Staple.

Cut length of bubble pack about 4.80m long. Stick to top of box.

Cut two side pieces of bubble pack as fig. 2.

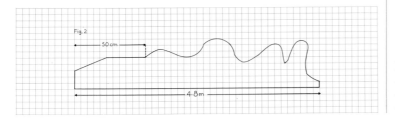

Fig. 2   50cm   4.8m

Glue these to sides of head, then staple to long top piece of bubble pack, curving the top up and down to fit the sides.

Make holes in tops of yoghurt cartons and insert spring with bobble attached into each. Paint with eye.

Make two holes in top of head and insert other two springs for antennae/ears. Wrap a little bubble pack around the springs and staple.

Add a further length of bubble pack for tail, then paint whole thing with the varnish (ordinary paint will not take). Add a couple of paper whiskers to either side of head.

Soda Fountain

Joanna David's English beauty brings a charm and elegance to every role she plays – certainly she was the best Rebecca I have ever seen. I was thrilled by the way this costume turned out – her prettiness transforms some strips of polythene packing material into a magic, bubbling fountain.

MATERIALS

(To fit adult, size 10–12)
3.3m water-coloured fabric, 92cm wide
11m bubble pack 60cm wide
4 paper plates
2.5m of 1.5cm elastic
corrugated cardboard
shirring elastic
copydex

Cut 1 piece of fabric as fig. 1.

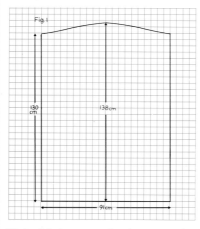

Right side in sew up back seam and turn right side out. Turn 3cm to inside along top edge and machine to form channel for elastic, leaving 5cm open for threading. Thread with elastic to fit around chest.

For shoulder frill, cut two 30cm deep strips across fabric, and for waist frill cut two 50cm strips across. Right sides together, join the pairs of pieces together into two long strips by stiching up the selvages. On both frills turn in and stitch channel for elastic as on dress.

Cut enough strips of bubble pack of varying lengths, between 50 and 120cm to encircle both frills. Staple each strip below elastic channels.

Measure elastic for shoulders and thread through the shorter frill. Measure elastic for waist and thread through the longer frill. Join both into circles.

For hat, copydex the bases of 2 paper plates together. Then fold 2 more paper plates in half and staple one to each side of underneath of the stuck pair at edges (fig. 2).

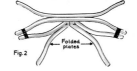

Gather up a 16cm deep strip of fabric along its edge and fit this frill between the 2 top plates and tack ends together.

Cut more strips of bubble pack and staple around outside edge of top plate. With shirring elastic in spool, stitch down the length of an 8cm wide strip of fabric, gathering it into a double-edged frill. Gather up more strips of bubble pack into the centre of the hat and wrap the frill around to secure and tack into place. Take a few more strips of bubble pack, wind a further strip around them to make them stand up and sellotape to top of hat. Staple elastic to underneath of hat to fit under chin.

Cut 2 pieces of corrugated cardboard as fig. 3, with the lines going in opposite directions for strength. Spread copydex on smooth sides and glue together.

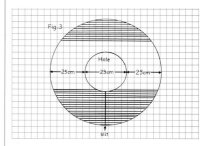

Cut 2 pieces of corrugated cardboard as fig. 4 and stick similarly. The circular piece fits around the waist, supporting the waist frill, and the oval piece fits over the head and sits around the shoulders to support the shoulder frill, both being worn over the fabric dress.

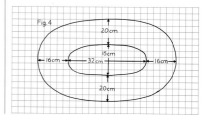

Pied Piper

If I was the pied piper I'm not at all sure I would want to be followed by this nasty collection of black rubber rats – and I can imagine the strings might become rather tiresome at a disco party . . . however it does make a very funny costume and is extremely simple to make.

MATERIALS

(To fit 8–10 year old)
hat (see p. 140) made in red or yellow
cotton, or half and half
jerkin as for Robin Hood, but made in
yellow and red cotton (p. 107)
shoes as for medieval boy (p. 28)
belt, red polo neck, yellow tights and
a pipe

black rubber rats, or homemade from
stuffed felt etc
string

Simply tie the strings around the rats and then attach the other ends to the back of the belt.

Newspiper | Clown

What a terrible pun! Probably most effective when used in conjunction with Pied Piper for two children or adults, but still very funny on its own. It won't last very long at a party but makes for a good entrance, and if you have as many old newspapers lying around your house as we always seem to, it won't cost a penny. I think the best part for Henrietta was ripping them all off afterwards.

MATERIALS

newspaper
safety pins, sellotape
pipe (or painted stick, etc.)

Simply tape and pin newspaper all over the piper, and make a hat in the way one folds a paper boat.

What a sweet little sad clown Zoe makes — and if you took the pom-poms off afterwards and put on pretty buttons or bows to hide the marks it would make a lovely party outfit.

MATERIALS

(To fit 5–6 year old)
3.3m shiny blue material 115cm wide
70cm shiny white material 115cm wide
1 cereal packet
elastic
bias binding
stapler

Cut 4 pieces as fig. 1 and cut 2 sleeves as fig. 2. Right sides together, join sleeves to body at armhole seams. Stitch centre front seam. Stitch underarm and side seams. Join inside leg seams. Stitch crutch seam to waist level at back, leave an opening of 33cm to neck. Gather up neck edge to fit neck.

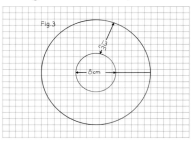

Make small hems at ends of sleeves then elasticate a few centimetres from end, to leave a frill. Make channel in trouser bottoms and thread with elastic.

FOR RUFF

Cut four circles in white as fig. 3. Cut an opening, and join all four pieces together end to end into one long circular strip by stitching them together at their open ends. Gather up the inside edge and fit round neck of suit. Bind off neck with bias binding. Add hook and eye.

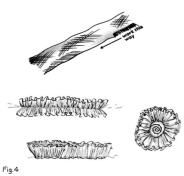

FOR POM-POMS

Cut strips of fabric on the cross 8cm wide and as long as possible. Fray edges by drawing a knife along the raw edges against the grain. When both edges are frayed, tightly gather up each strip down the middle then fold in half widthwise and machine along the fold line (fig. 4)

Fig.4

Cut lengths of the gathered strip approx. 12cm and roll up, securing as you go with needle and cotton.

FOR THE HAT

Bend the opened up cereal packet into a cone. Trim bottom edge as necessary and secure with staples. Cover the shape with white fabric and add pom-pom (as above, but rolled-up before the folding in half stage, to make it more three-dimensional).

Scotch Egg

Another pleasing pun — and a good way to vary an existing costume. You could also of course use the hat, sash and sporran with a little kilt as a Scotsman's outfit.

MATERIALS

(To fit 4–6 year old)
egg as for Humpty Dumpty (but could be left white)
30cm tartan fabric 115cm wide
scraps brown fur fabric, brown felt and white fur
30cm black felt 90cm wide
feather ends
gold button

Cut purse shape from brown fur fabric. Cut 3 strips of brown felt, 20cm by 4cm, slash and roll up to form tassels and tack to secure. Stitch each onto thin felt strips, 6cm long and staple in V formation to centre of sporran. Stitch strips of felt or tape to sides for tying around hips. Staple 3 pieces of white fur above tassels.

Cut 2 circles of black felt 30cm diameter, and stitch together around edge. Cut central hole in one circle 18cm diameter and turn right side out. Cut a strip of felt 3cm deep and stitch around edge of hole. Staple bits of fur and feather ends to beret and add gold button or brooch (fig. 1).

Fig.1

Pin tartan as sash.

Humpty-Dumpty

Little Damion looks so sweet as an egg that I hate to think of it breaking to pieces – let's hope this one keeps well away from any high walls.

MATERIALS

(To fit 4–6 year old)
1 small and 1 large paper lampshade
card
spray paints
magic marker
60cm white jersey, 115cm wide
white gloves
stapler
scraps for bow-tie

Hang lampshades on a line and spray with paint. When dry cut a hole in small shade for face and then staple to large shade as fig. 1.

Cut armholes. Keep hanging all the time to prevent squashing. Make collar out of card and staple round join, trying to hide the curving in of both shades (fig. 2).

Paint waistline, buttons and checks onto body, either with a stencil and spray paint or by hand with emulsion. Add a fabric bow tie.

FOR LEGGINGS

Cut 2 strips of the jersey and draw checks with the magic marker. Make stencil of a square and spray to match body or paint by hand. When dry stitch seam at back to make stockings.

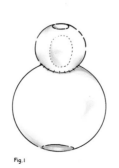

Fig.1

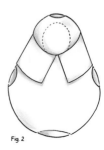

Fig.2

ZODIAC

As an Aries myself, I thoroughly approve of a strong, talented character like Alan Price representing us. It's not that I believe in all that nonsense of course, but still . . .

MATERIALS

50cm white fleece 115cm wide
2 coat hangers
steel wool
scrap of wadding
remnant white voile or chiffon
narrow white cord
sheepskin coat

Make fleece balaclava (see p. 140).

Cut 4 ear shapes from fleece as fig. 1.

Right sides together, stitch around each pair of ears, leaving bottom open. Turn right sides out.

Straighten out wire coat hangers and twist both together, tapering to points at ends. Wrap steel wool around the hangers, leaving a 22cm gap in the middle. Wind 10cm wide strip of voile around the steel wool covered ends, tack in place then wind narrow cord around the voile and tie at base (fig. 2).

Wrap wadding around central wire piece and tack. Cut strip of fur fabric to fit over wadding and tack in place. Twist ends into spirals (fig. 3).

Stitch central fur of horns into place on balaclava. Fold ears in half and stitch below horns. Wear with coat.

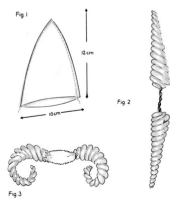

Fig. 1

12 cm

10cm

Fig. 2

Fig. 3

Taurus

This is Jill Thraves, whose invaluable assistance made this book possible. If being a Taurus means having bull-like determination, then thank goodness she is one.

MATERIALS

50cm black fur fabric 115cm wide
wire coat hanger
wadding
black spray paint
steel wool
black coat and trousers

Make very loose fur balaclava (see p. 140).

Cut 4 ear shapes (fig. 1).

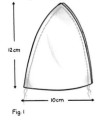

Fig. I

Right sides together, stitch around each pair of ears, leaving bottom open. Turn right side out.

From the wire coat hanger, fashion basic horn shape, twisting two thicknesses together for strength (fig. 2).

Fig. 2

Wrap steel wool around horns, tapering towards ends. Spray with black paint. Wrap wadding around central wire piece and tack in place. Cover with a strip of black fur and stitch into place on the balaclava. Fold ears in half lengthwise and stitch beneath horns.

Cut tail from remaining fur fabric as fig. 3.

Fig. 3

Spread wrong side with copydex, fold in half lengthwise and stick.

Wear suitable black clothes – leather looks very good – and attach tail.

Gemini

Do make sure you choose someone you get on well with when you wear this costume, or it could be a very nasty evening. Luckily Araminta and Daisy are great friends, and got very giggly when we were taking the photographs. Of course it could also be a good way of getting to know someone – fast.

MATERIALS

(To fit two 12–15 year olds)
2 old curtains, or 2m of fabric, 115cm wide
another curtain for shirt, or 2m of fabric 115cm wide
elastic
scrap for bow-tie
shirt buttons

Fold the curtain or shirt fabric and cut out as fig. 1.

Right sides together, sew underarm and side seams, add buttons if desired.

For trousers, fold each curtain in half lengthwise and cut out each leg as fig. 2.

Right sides together, sew crutch seams to join legs together. Sew inside leg seams. Turn right side out and turn over top to inside to form channel for elastic, leaving opening for threading. Stitch, then thread with enough elastic to go round both people. Add fabric bow-tie.

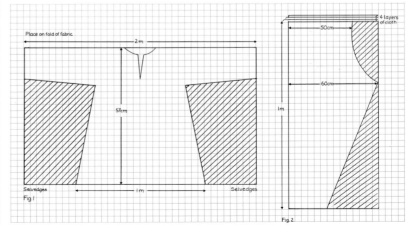

Cancer

I suppose this is what they call a 'soft shell' crab: you could always make a firmer one if you wanted by using cardboard inside (see Valentine Heart, p. 17). I rather liked the idea of it being a sort of soft sculpture – and the pinky colour makes my good friend Geraldine Garner look good enough to eat.

MATERIALS

(To fit size 10)
1.4m pale pink lining fabric 91cm wide
2.8m dark pink lining fabric, 91cm wide
4m medium weight wadding headband with balls on springs scraps for eyes
thread or wool

Cut one shape in dark pink, one in pale and 2 in wadding (fig. 1).

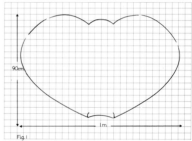

Fig. 1

Cut one shape in pale pink and one in wadding (fig. 2).

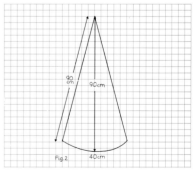

Fig. 2

Stitch wadding to wrong sides of both body pieces, around outside edge. Stitch wadding to wrong side of triangular inset piece.

Cut 4 pieces in dark pink and 4 in wadding (fig. 5).

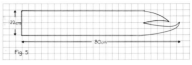

Fig. 5

Stitch wadding to wrong side of each piece around edges.

Right sides together, stitch both pairs of leg pieces together leaving end open. Turn right side out.

Cut 2 holes 44cm circumference in pale front body piece where wearer's arms should come out – see fig. 3 – and stitch open end of each leg into each hole leg seams top and bottom.

Cut 8 pieces of dark pink and 8 pieces of wadding (fig. 6).

Fig. 6

Stitch wadding to wrong side of each piece. Fold along dotted line (fig. 6) right sides out and stitch up the side, using zig-zag stitch.

Stitch legs together in pairs (fig. 7).

Open out each pair and sew to centre front one above the other (fig. 8).

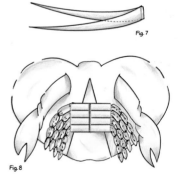

Fig. 7

Fig. 8

Tie strong thread or wool around each leg in 3 places to create sections (fig. 8).

For headdress cover balls with pink fabric and then glue on scraps for eyes. Cut slits in fabric at wrists to allow hands out for holding drinks, etc.!

Slit paler body shape up centre, and stitch the triangular inset into the opening, sides together (fig. 3).

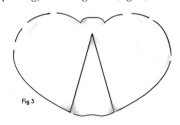

Fig. 3

Place the two crab body shapes together, wadding on inside, and stitch together round edge, leaving 30cm open at top for head, and 45cm open at bottom for legs. Stitch as shown to make crab markings (fig. 4).

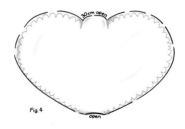

Fig. 4

Leo

Not the most frightening of lions –
it reminds me rather of the
cowardly lion in The Wizard of
Oz – but Mike makes it very
cuddly looking. The simple
costume is easy to make, very
comfortable, and can be the basis
for many variations (see Hare,
p. 92, and Sagittarius, p. 61).

MATERIALS

(To fit large adult)

1.3m of brown (lion-coloured)
    polyester 152cm wide
2 mop heads
80cm waist elastic
scraps of wadding, old tights etc. for
    stuffing

Cut two shapes in brown fabric (fig.
1).

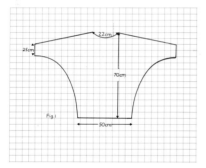

Right sides together, stitch underarm
seams and top arm seams.

Cut 2 trouser pieces (fig. 2).

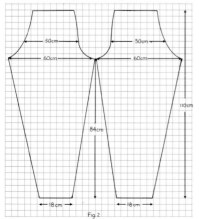

Right sides together, stitch inside leg
seams in each piece. Turn each leg
right side out. Matching inside leg
seams, with right sides together stitch
seam C (fig. 3).

Turn 3cm to inside at waist edge and
machine to form channel for elastic,
leaving 5cm open for threading.
Thread with elastic.

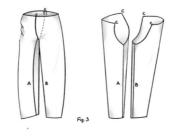

Make balaclava in brown fabric (see
p. 140).

Cut 4 ear shapes (fig. 4).

Right sides together, join ear shapes
in pairs, stitching around outside
edges as shown, leaving bottom edge
open. Turn right side out. On each
ear, make a little pleat in the centre,
bringing points A and B together.
Turn fold to the side and stitch along
bottom edge. Stitch ears onto
balaclava.

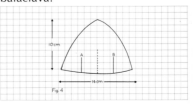

Remove mop string from its metal clasps, straighten out and cut lengths into four. Placing these very close together, attach to balaclava in rows, working from face edge down to neck edge, avoiding ears, stitching down centre of strands. Cover whole head (fig. 5).

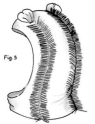

Fig. 5

Attach neck edge of balaclava to neck opening of body.

Cut one piece in brown fabric for tail (fig. 6).

6 cm
110 cm
Fig. 6

Fold down centre, right side in, and stitch up side leaving end open. Turn right side out and lightly stuff with wadding, rags, tights etc. Stitch several short lengths of mop string to end. Attach to back of trousers.

Draw around outline of hand and thumb to make pattern for mittens. Cut 4, and, right sides together, join into pairs, stitching around outer edge. Turn right side out.

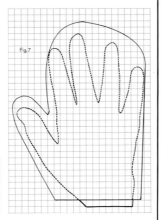

Fig. 7

Libra

Shirley Freeman looks very beautiful in her simple white shift. For a long time she has been a successful career woman, and now that she has produced a beautiful baby daughter I imagine, like Libra, she has her life in perfect balance.

MATERIALS

(To fit adult)
material as for Greek Lady (p. 27) plus
*   Greek Man's tunic (p. 27)*
cardboard
2 paper bowls
silver chain
silver foil
strong thread

Cut a shape from card for top of scales and cover with foil. Attach three lengths of chain to each end by tying with strong thread. Cover the bowls with silver foil and join chains to them with more thread.

Wear material as for Greek Lady around waist, and as for Greek Man pinned or tied at shoulders. Tack or pin side seams.

Virgo

Let's face it – this is not an easy star sign to represent nowadays without inspiring some very unwitty remarks and the occasional smirk. Flora looks sweet and innocent enough to play it straight, and as her lamp is obviously full of oil I'm glad to see she is a wise one as well.

MATERIALS

(To fit adult)
costume as for Greek Boy and Girl
*   (p. 27)*
millinery wire
tissue paper and sellotape
lamp

Simply wear the Greek Boy's tunic over the Greek Girl's shift with the girl's peplum on top. Tack up sides. Make some paper flowers by scrunching up pieces of tissue paper and taping onto millinery wire bent into a circle to fit the head. Carry lamp.

Scorpio

This lining fabric makes a wonderfully shiny Scorpion – and the sunglasses give the eyes a very insecty look. Although it looks quite complicated it's not as difficult to make as it seems.

MATERIALS

(To fit size 12–14)

4m black 'satin' lining fabric
1.6m fabric for lining 115cm wide
4m medium weight wadding 115cm wide
black cord or wool
trousers as for Father Christmas (p. 128) but black, cut short and elasticated
Cut 2 shapes as fig. 1 in black satin, 2 in wadding and 2 in lining.

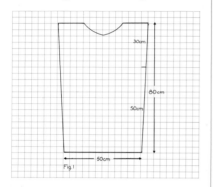

Sandwich wadding between satin (right side out) and lining. Stitch around edge through all three thicknesses.

Divide bottom 50cm of each piece into seven sections and stitch across through all three thicknesses. Stitch curve at shoulders similarly (fig. 2).

Right sides together, match markings, stitch shoulder seams and side seams, leaving armholes open (fig. 2).

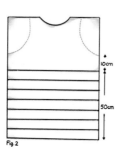

Fold remaining fabric and cut 4 shapes in black satin and 4 in wadding (fig. 3).

Stitch wadding to wrong side of each satin shape. Divide each piece into 3 equal parts and stitch across, as fig. 3.

Right sides together, stitch leg pieces

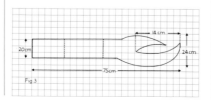

into pairs around edges, leaving ends open. Turn right sides out.

Gather armholes to fit raw edges of each leg and matching shoulder seams and underarm seams to seams in legs stitch into armholes.

Cut 8 shapes in satin and 8 in wadding (fig. 4).

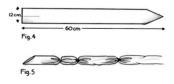

Stitch wadding to back of each satin leg, fold lengthwise and stitch up side with zig-zag.

Tie strong cord or wool around each leg at intervals as shown in fig. 5. Stitch across end for 'foot'.

Join legs at edges A into 4 pairs.

Stitch side by side down centre front, tacking also at first joint (fig. 6).

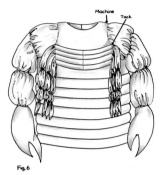

Fig.6

Make opening in back neck, big enough to allow head in. Finish raw edges and fasten with hook and eye.

Make balaclava from satin backed with wadding (see p. 140) but with slight variation in shape (fig. 7).

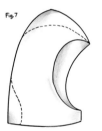

Fig.7

Cut one shape in satin and one in wadding (fig. 8).

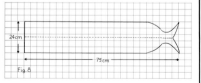

24cm

75cm

Fig.8

Stitch wadding to wrong side of satin around edge. Fold lengthwise, right side in, and stitch around edge, leaving end open. Turn right side out. Divide into six sections by tying with cord or wool. Stitch open end to centre back lower edge of body. Tack pointed end about 30cm up back.

Cut slits in fabric of both wrists to allow hands out to hold drinks, etc.!

Sagittarius

Poor Rodney Bewes, having suffered the indignity of wearing my 'Submarine Commander' (p. 86), gamely stripped off when I discovered he was a Sagittarius. I love the way actors plunge themselves wholeheartedly into a role – even when half naked and wearing a horse's tail.

MATERIALS

legs as for Lion (p. 58)
1 mop head
bow and arrow (or cut one out of card)

Simply prise open metal clip of mop and straighten out strands into long lengths. Bunch together to form a tail and tack to back of trousers.

Capricorn

I got into the habit of casually asking my friends what Zodiac sign they were when they came to be photographed for the book, and when I found Susannah York was a Capricorn I press-ganged her straight from being an angel fish into a goat. Certainly nothing silly about this one – and how many girls would look so pretty wearing a beard?

MATERIALS

50cm white fur fabric 115cm wide
scrap long-haired fur fabric
coat hanger
steel wool
scrap wadding
remnant white voile or chiffon
narrow cord
white jumper and tights

Make loose balaclava from white fur fabric (see p. 140). Cut 4 ear shapes as fig. 1.

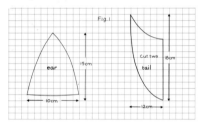

Right sides together, stitch around each pair of ears, leaving bottom open. Turn right sides out.

From one wire coat hanger, fashion basic horns shape, twisting two thicknesses together for strength (fig. 2).

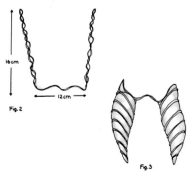

Wrap steel wool around the two horns, tapering to tips (fig. 3).

Wrap wadding around centre piece and tack in place. Wind 10cm wide strips of voile around horns and tack in place. Wind narrow cord around horns from tip to base and tie.

Make two holes in balaclava towards front of head 12cm apart, big enough to poke horns through. Push them through then tack at centre and round base of horns to secure.

Fold both ears in half lengthwise, position below horns and tack in place (fig. 4).

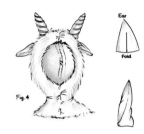

Make triangular beard from long-haired fabric, position below chin and tack onto either side of balaclava (or it can be stuck to the chin with a little safe adhesive).

For tail, cut two pieces of fur fabric as fig. 1.

Right sides together, stitch around two edges, leaving third side open. Fig. 5. Turn right side out, lightly stuff and tack open side together.

Wear white jumper and tights/trousers, and pin or tack tail in position.

Aquarius

I thought for a time about having real water in the vase that Julian is holding and taking the picture just as it poured out, but then decided that would not be very practical either for taking to a party nor for the floor of the photographer's studio. The paper strips make a more suitable replacement.

MATERIALS

Grecian looking tunic (see Greek Lady, p. 27)
vase
strips of blue shiny paper
sellotape
gold headband (see Greek Man, p. 27)
sandals

The Greek Lady's tunic described on page 27 makes a perfect length of tunic for an adult. Stick strips of blue paper to the inside of the vase and wear the gold headband and sandals.

Pisces

This looks extremely attractive on a pretty girl like Linda, and very pleasingly mimics the Pisces symbol. If you were feeling really brave you could just stick the top with safe glue or toupee tape in strategic places, instead of pinning it to the bikini.

MATERIALS

(To fit adult)
1m fishy fabric 115cm wide
60cm wadding, medium
2 pearl sequins
2 black sequins
bikini

Fold fabric in two and cut 4 fish shapes as fig. 1 in fish fabric and two in wadding.

To make each fish, sandwich the wadding between the two fabric shapes, right side out. Stitch through all three thicknesses around outline, then stitch lines onto fins, and mouth, gill and scales onto body (fig. 2).

For eyes, use large pearlised sequins with small black ones glued in the centre. Glue one to the left side of one fish, and the other to the right side of the second fish. Place the fish facing opposite directions and tack their tails together.

Wear the bikini and with the fishes tails centre back wrap one fish around the bikini top and the other around the bottom and tack in place.

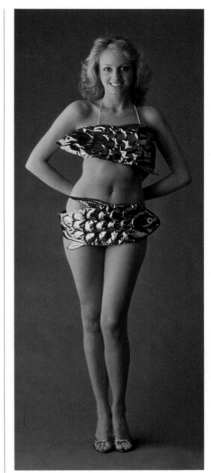

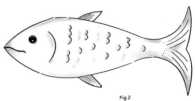

Fig 2

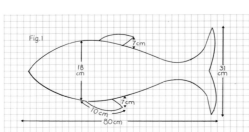

Fig. 1

Ladybird

I saw this lovely spotted shiny material and couldn't resist making a ladybird. Really of course the spots are a bit small, and you could just as easily make it with plain red fabric and glue on a few spots – but who's going to worry if it looks as sweet as it does here on little Martha?

MATERIALS

(To fit 2–4 year old)
70cm soft black fabric 90cm wide
70cm red spotted fabric 115cm wide
70cm medium weight wadding
4.8m rigilene or corrugated
cardboard
2 pipe cleaners, painted black
1 pair black tights
black pop socks or long black gloves

Cut one shape in black fabric as fig. 1.

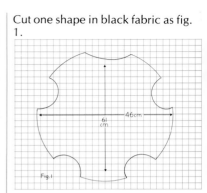

Fig.1

Using 1.75m of ridgilene form an oval to match outline of black shape, stapling or sewing ends together. Using 4 more lengths of ridgilene construct shell shape onto the oval (fig. 2) or make shell shape from corrugated cardboard as for Tortoise (p. 92)

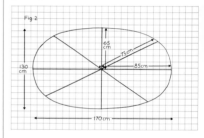

Fig. 2

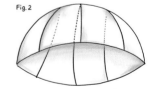

Fig. 2

Cover the shell shape with wadding and then with spotted fabric, making tucks and darts as necessary. Sew black under piece to shell, leaving shoulders open.

Make black balaclava (see p. 140) and staple black pipe cleaners to top for antennae.

Secure shoulders with hooks and eyes, or safety pins. Wear black tights and pop socks or gloves on arms.

Caterpillar

I've never been frightened by any kind of 'creepy-crawly' and have always particularly liked the furry looking type of caterpillar. Verity makes a charming one, and adopted a marvellous position for our cover — it would be wonderful to crawl into a party like that through the front door.

MATERIALS

(To fit 8–10 year old)
4.6m green fabric, 91m wide
scraps of black fur and orange felt
2 pipe cleaners
7 pairs black pop socks
shirring elastic
rags, kapok, newspapers for stuffing

Cut a 4.20m length of green fabric. From one end mark with pins or chalk at edges 12 widths of 15cm. Starting from the other end measure off in the same way 12 widths of 20cm (fig. 1).

Fig.1

With wider spaced marks towards you, bring bottom edge up to meet top edge. Pin across at marked widths, matching marks on layers of fabric, to form folds (see Palm Tree, p. 22). Thread bobbin of machine with shirring elastic and stitch along pinned lines twice for strength. You now have a 'lining' with folds on top. Sew up side seam, right sides together, forming tube. Make balaclava out of remaining green fabric (see p. 140). Gather top of body onto neck of balaclava and shirr. Stuff 5 pairs of pop socks with kapok, rags or old newspapers and attach to body at second, fourth, seventh, ninth and tenth segments, counting head as first segment. Make holes for arms and feet in third and eighth. Wear remaining pop socks on arms and feet. Decorate caterpillar with scraps as desired.

Sandwich Man

Club Sandwich

Ham Sandwich

I have known Martin Shaw since working with him in 'Look Back in Anger' at the Royal Court Theatre many years ago. He is an extremely fine actor, and here brings to the demanding role of a sandwich a subtlety and depth that would be the envy of many a packed lunch. It's a light, easy costume to wear, enormous fun to make, and there must be many more variations if you put your mind to it.

MATERIALS

2 pieces strong card about 90cm
square
1.8m thick wadding
red crêpe paper or red fabric
remnants
white and yellow crêpe or fabric
remnants
white pipe cleaners
green crêpe or remnants
webbing and tape
brown paint spray
copydex

Cut wadding to fit two pieces of card and copydex one piece onto each card. Spray edges brown to suggest crust.

For shoulder straps cut 2 lengths of webbing each about 80cm and attach to backs of cards as shown with glue and staple gun.

Cut 4 lengths of tape about 40cm each and staple also to backs of cards (fig. 1).

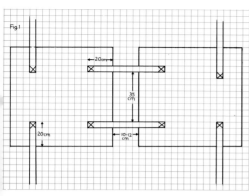

Fig.1

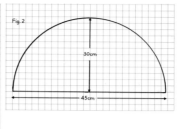

Fig.2

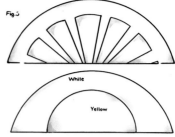

Fig.3

White

Yellow

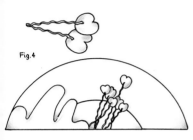

Fig.4

Cut 8 shapes in cardboard (fig. 2).

Cover some in red fabric or crêpe and mark with red felt tip as tomatoes. Cover others with white and yellow like hardboiled egg (fig. 3).

Cut tiny bits of green crêpe for cress. Glue onto egg and tomato pieces with pipe cleaners for stalks (or staple). Add shaped bits of yellow for mayonnaise (fig. 4).

Arrange tomato and egg pieces around outer edge of front sandwich half and glue or staple behind. Add pieces of green 'lettuce' behind these.

Tie tapes at sides when wearing, and add extra crêpe lettuce to fill in sides.

Add props for sandwich variations as desired.

Toasted Sandwich

Chicken Sandwich

Sandwich spread

Cheese Sandwich

Open Sandwich

BIRDS

Stool Pigeon

A pleasing pun, and worn by one of my favourite actors – James Coburn, who was pounced on for the photograph when here for something quite different (see p. 134). He certainly makes a very handsome pigeon.

MATERIALS

1 roll white lavatory paper
1 papier mâché head shape (see p. 140)
grey spray paint
small piece corrugated cardboard scraps for eyes
shirring elastic
stapler
sellotape
white paint
glue

Using shirring elastic in the bobbin of your machine, stitch down the edge of a few metres of the paper. Beginning at the back, stretch lengths of paper across the head shape, stapling at sides and taping where necessary. Overlap each row by about half its width, roughly following dotted lines (fig. 1).

Fig. 1

Smooth the last piece of paper over the front end and tuck gathered edge under rim of papier mâché. Glue this last piece to the previous one to make it smooth (fig. 2).

Inside

Fig. 2

Spray grey.

Cut 4 upper and lower beak pieces, 2 of each shape, in corrugated cardboard (fig. 3).

69

Swallow

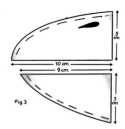

Staple the two top pieces together along upper edge and staple the lower pieces together along lower edge (fig. 3).

Paint white and mark nostril with felt tip on either side of top beak. Overlap bottom half of beak by top beak and staple together as shown (fig. 4).

Place beak at front of head, splay edges out and staple down.

Cut 2 eye shapes from scrap of orange material and 2 pupils from black. Glue pupils to eyes and eyes to head.

Take a stool with you or borrow one at the party!

Gemma Craven turned up looking so pretty in her red mini skirt and striped top that I was determined to take a photograph of her as she was, as well as in her Nell Gwynne costume (p. 117). I concocted this bird for her on the spot – a nicely silly pun.

MATERIALS

feet as for Grouse (p. 71)
cardboard
black bin liner
glue
couple of feathers
glass of water

Cut swallow tail shape from cardboard and cover with black plastic from bin liner. Grip a couple of feathers in the hair, and wear feet. Hold a glass of water as if permanently about to swallow!

Grouse

If you put on a really complaining expression as Frazer Hines has for our photograph, then this makes another good pun – it also might make a change from having to be the life and soul of a party all evening.

MATERIALS

papier mâché headpiece as p. 140
white lavatory paper
brown spray paint or brown crêpe
red and black scraps for eyes
cardboard
white paint
orange fabric or crêpe paper for feet

Cover head shape with lavatory paper (or 10cm deep strips of crêpe paper) as for Stool Pigeon (see p. 69). Spray brown if necessary.

Cut 2 red shapes for eyes and glue black pupils onto them as fig. 1.

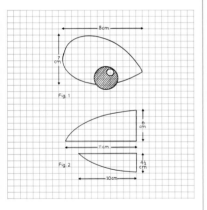

Cut 4 cardboard shapes 2 top and 2 bottom as fig. 2.

Paint white and then staple into beak shapes and onto head as Stool Pigeon (p. 69).

Glue eyes onto head.

Using 3 lengths of lavatory paper of 3 sheets each, stitch together side by side and gather into narrow fan shape. Stitch across end (fig. 3).

Make feet in cardboard and orange fabric as for Jail Bird (p. 72).

Cut two rectangles of corrugated cardboard 44cm × 26cm. Stitch twelve 50cm lengths of paper with shirring elastic as for head, then tape 6 lengths to each cardboard piece overlapping as for head. Spray with brown paint. Tape or staple round legs.

Jail Bird

From the way Martin Shaw so skilfully assumed a criminal look when he put on this costume, it almost seemed as if it was a relief to be on the wrong side of the law after his years as a 'goody' in 'The Professionals'. I'm sure no prisoner anywhere any longer has to suffer the indignity of arrows all over him but as in a cartoon it immediately creates an effect.

MATERIALS

1 papier mâché headpiece (see p. 140)
1 packet yellow crêpe paper
1 packet brown crêpe paper or brown material
cardboard
scraps of orange and black material or paper for eyes
thick black felt tip pen
stapler
sellotape
glue
beach ball

Cut strips of yellow crêpe 10cm deep and cover the headpiece as in Stool Pigeon (p. 69). Decorate with black felt tip arrows.

Cut 2 orange circles for eyes and glue a black circle in the centre of each. Cut upper and lower lid for each eye and glue eyes and lids onto head.

Cut 2 of each shape in cardboard and 2 of each shape in brown material (fig. 1).

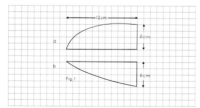

Glue brown fabric onto cardboard shapes and staple together as for Stool Pigeon. Staple onto front of head.

Gather a strip of crêpe 20cm deep into fan shape for tail, and mark with black arrows (fig. 2).

For feet, cut 2 shapes in cardboard (fig. 3).

Place each foot shape onto brown fabric and cut around outside allowing 3cm extra all around edge. Staple fabric onto card, pushing extra fabric into the centre to allow for

Fig. 2

height of foot. Make a slit in the fabric of each to allow foot to push in.

Make a chain from ovals of cardboard slit and joined together and spray black. Add a beach ball covered or sprayed black.

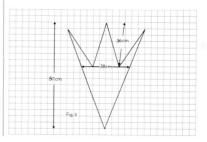

Secretary Bird

My sister Clare makes a very efficient looking secretary bird. This could be fun for an office party – but it wouldn't be too easy to sit on the boss's knee with those long tail feathers . . .

MATERIALS

1 papier mâché head shape (p. 140)
pale blue lavatory paper
small amount yellow crêpe paper
1 packet black crêpe paper
orange scraps for eyes
cardboard
white paint
pink felt or crêpe paper for feet
pink ribbon

Cover head shape with lavatory paper as for Stool Pigeon (p. 69).

Cut shape in yellow crêpe as fig. 1.

Turn edge A under front edge of headpiece and staple. Glue rest of shape to head. Cut 2 orange circles for eyes and add black pupils and lids and glue to head (fig. 1).

Cut 2 lengths of black crêpe, 30cm long. Fold in half and machine down every 4cm. Slash between stitching lines (fig. 2).

Staple these 'feathers' to head on either side.

Cut 4 cardboard pieces, 2 in each shape as fig. 3.

Paint all 4 white and staple together as for Stool Pigeon. Mark nostril.

Cut 2 lengths of cardboard as fig. 4.

Cover both with lavatory paper and stick a strip of black crêpe paper 10cm wide 6cm from curved end. Staple together at straight ends not directly on top of each other but slightly fanned out.

Make feet from cardboard and pink felt as for Jail Bird (p. 72) but smaller and neater. Add pink ribbons to tie round ankles.

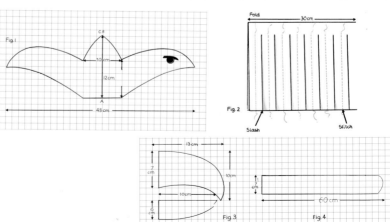

Six Pretty Flowers

These worked so successfully that they have become almost my favourite costumes. The children look so sweet and angelic in them one can't imagine that they behave in any way other than quite beautifully . . .

I have shown two ways of making the petals; in crêpe paper and in felt. The crêpe looks just as good and is cheaper, but obviously if you want them to last a long time then felt is better.

MATERIALS

(To fit child)
For each flower:
1m green felt, 90cm wide for head
  and leaves
1 packet suitably coloured crêpe
  paper (except for pansy)
black pipe cleaners for poppy
1 flower pot, base circumference
  roughly hip measurement
velcro
green polo neck
brown tights

For pansy only:
40cm yellow felt
30cm purple felt

For each flower make a green felt balaclava (see p. 140).

CORNFLOWER

Cut a strip of blue crêpe about 20cm wide. Stitch around face edge of balaclava, gathering as you go, so that it's very frilly. Makes slashes 5–8cm deep close together around outer edge (fig. 1).

Fig 1

DAFFODIL

Cut strip of yellow crêpe 18cm wide. Stitch around face edge of balaclava, barely gathering, so that it stands out forwards. Stitch another strip of paper behind the first, gathering more as you go so that it forms a frill (fig. 2). Cut this frill into 5 petal shapes.

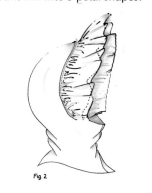

Fig 2

POPPY

Cut a strip of red crêpe 20cm wide. Stitch around face edge of balaclava, gathering as you go. Stitch a second frill behind this one. Cut the first frill nearest face into two petal shapes, one on each side of face, and the second frill also into two petals, at top and bottom. Cut through the centre of the bottom petal to allow opening for head (fig. 3). Gently stretch crêpe at edges to resemble poppy. Staple black pipe cleaners around face edge.

Fig 3

ROSE

Cut lengths of pink crêpe paper about 25cm long and 18cm deep. Cut top corners into curves (fig. 4).

Stitch these around face edge, overlapping each by about 8–10cm,

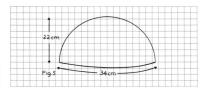

Fig 4

gathering as you go. Make 3–4 rows of petals. Gently stretch edge of each petal to resemble rose.

PANSY

Cut 2 purple and 3 yellow petals in felt (fig. 5).

Make 3 tucks in lower edge of each petal to reduce measurement to 18cm. Stitch two yellow ones on either side of face, pointing forwards from face edge, with folds pointing downwards. Stitch the two purple petals at the top, placing each slightly behind its neighbouring yellow petal. Stitch halfway across the last yellow petal on one side of face edge below chin. The other half will fasten across with velcro behind yellow petal on other side.

Lightly tack edges of petals to each other for support.

HAREBELL

Cut a strip of blue crêpe paper about 18cm wide and sew around face edge, gathering as you go. Cut into 5 pointed petal shapes. Gently stretch edges of petals. Cut out 2 shapes of green felt as fig. 6. Gather a 14cm

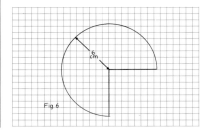

Daisies

Although it doesn't appear so to the observer, one can in fact see quite clearly through the yellow centre of each daisy. You could always leave it open of course, like the children's flowers but the veiled look is quite mysterious and very effective.

MATERIALS

plastic flower pot, base
  circumference roughly hip
  measurement
white buckram 40cm × 91cm
1.6m green felt 90cm wide
40cm transparent yellow fabric
1.6m tape 25mm wide
70cm of 4cm elastic
brown fabric remnant for 'soil'
glue
stanley knife and/or hacksaw
velcro

Cut 12 petals in buckram as fig. 1. Colour by painting if desired.

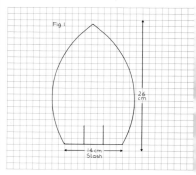

Make 2 slashes 2cm deep at base of each petal, and fold the 3 flaps thus formed alternately forward and back (fig. 2). Attach the 12 petals onto 60cm of 25.4mm tape overlapping to fit. Stitch on either side of petals to secure all the flaps (fig. 2).

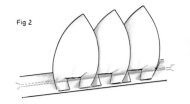

Fig 2

wide strip of crêpe around the edge of each shape 3cm from the edge (fig. 7). Cut the edge of the felt into 5 even 'sepal' shapes, then cut the crêpe into 5 petal shapes. Join the straight edges to make bell shapes. Sew little strips of felt onto each to make stalks (fig. 8).

To adapt flower pots for wearing, see Daisies.

LEAVES

Cut two shapes of green felt for each flower as fig. 9. Vary shape as desired for different flowers.

Fig 7

Wear green polo necks, brown tights, flower pots and flower headdresses, pinned or 'velcro'd under chin. Tack or safety pin leaves around sleeves, and for harebell tack little flowers onto sleeves or hold in each hand.

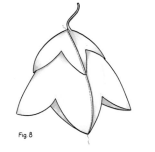

Fig 8

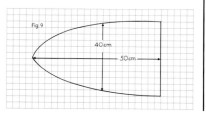

Fig 9

40cm

50cm

Cut length of felt 60cm long, with 12 shaped sepals 10cm deep and stitch to tape behind petals, matching each sepal to a petal (fig. 3).

Fig.3

Cut and sew a balaclava out of green felt (see p. 140).

Cut circle of yellow fabric 31cm diameter. Gather edge of circle onto face edge of balaclava 20cm down each side from centre forehead, leaving a 26cm gap on lower edge of yellow circle. Turn under this edge and thread with 15cm of narrow elastic (fig. 4).

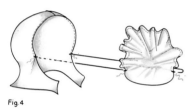

Fig.4

Now stitch tape with petals around edge of yellow centre having ends meet under chin. Fasten with velcro.

Cut two leaf shapes 80cm long and 60cm wide as fig. 5. Cut two further pieces 31cm long, tapering from 10cm width to a leaf point. Stitch around edges of the latter pieces onto leaf shapes to form central channels for arms.

Cut bottom out of plastic flower pot with stanley knife and hacksaw if necessary. Cut four lengths of tape to reach from bottom of pot to waist. Attach at equal intervals top ends of tapes to 4cm wide elastic to go around waist. Glue bottom ends to bottom edge of pot on the inside.

Cut circle of brown fabric of slightly larger circumference than pot and cut a circle in the centre to fit waist. This will be the 'soil'. Tuck it into waist elastic, or pin, and glue outside edge to inside of pot.

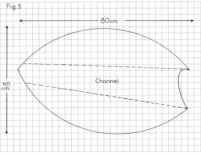

Fig.5

80cm

60 cm

Channel

Tarzan and Jane

A lovely easy couple of outfits to make, and as long as it's summer or there's some efficient central heating, very comfortable as well.

MATERIALS

(To fit adults)
90cm leopard fabric
velcro

FOR TARZAN

Cut piece of fabric roughly as fig. 1.

Overlap around hips and fasten with safety pin or velcro.

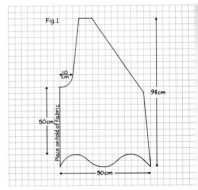

FOR JANE

Cut two pieces as fig. 2.

Tie the shorter one around bust and the other around hips.

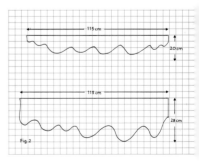

The Blob

When I asked Terry Jones if there was anything particular he would like to be for the book, he immediately said he would like to be a 'sex object', having always wondered exactly what such an object would look like. He had in mind something faintly surrealist and symbolic and although I had grave doubts about exactly what it should be like, I think the end result is really quite successful. He certainly made us all laugh while he was being photographed – but then Terry could make me laugh whatever he wore. I also made him a more conventional alternative 'sex object' costume (p. 108).

MATERIALS

6 1.8m lengths of 60cm wide bubble
   pack
4 1.8m lengths white wincyette
   115cm wide
sellotape
copydex
stapler

Make a front and a back from lengths of bubble pack sellotaped together to give a height of about 1.8m and width about 1.5m. Cut an irregular outline of bulges and curves and a hole in the front to fit the face. Stick white fabric all over this strange shape with copydex and add trimming as desired. Create more bulges and hollows by stapling tucks at random on the inside.

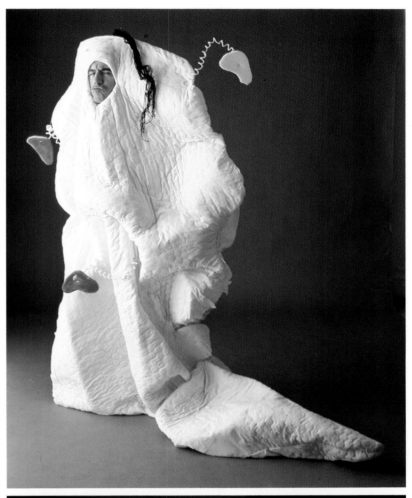

Statue on a Pill

MATERIALS

(To fit adult)
corrugated cardboard
plain cardboard
stanley knife
white paint and spray grey paint
glue
clothes as for Greek girl (p. 27)
pieces of ivy
stapler

Make a tube from corrugated cardboard with ridges outside and vertical about 1m circumference and 1.10m height. Staple. Cut two circles 1.75m circumference and two circles of 1.40m circumference out of cardboard. Cut hole in the middle of all of them of 14cm radius. Score a line 3cm away from these holes and slit the inside edge, then bend to form tabs (fig. 1).

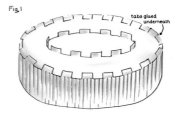

Fig. 1

tabs glued underneath

Cut two strips of corrugated cardboard 8cm by 1.75m, and two strips 8cm by 1.40m. Turn over by scoring and slitting 2cm along one edge of each strip to form tabs. Glue these strips around edges of cardboard circles as fig. 1. Then glue these in place on the top and bottom of the pillar (fig. 2).

Paint the pillar white and spray with a little grey paint. Stick some real ivy here and there. Wear the Greek robe and slide into the pillar upwards.

Jill Townsend looks so remarkably cool and beautiful in this costume that for a moment or two I think it quite fools the eye into seeing a real statue. I admit it may not be the easiest of outfits to walk in – although it is possible – but if anyone wishes to put their lady on a pedestal . . . here's how.

Pea Pod

I love fresh peas and look forward to their arrival each year as a sign of summer on the way: somehow the work of shelling them makes them taste extra delicious. Certainly Zoe looks as sweet as they taste in this costume – rather like a fairy drawn by Arthur Rackham.

MATERIALS

(To fit 4–6 year old)
3m green felt 90cm wide
3.6m rigilene
2.4m narrow black elastic
4 medium size rubber footballs

Cut 2 shapes in green felt as fig. 1.

Fig.I

|← 1·20m →|

Stitch together down back seam as shown. Open out and stitch a length of rigilene down this seam on the inside. Stitch two more lengths of rigilene to inside of both open edges.

Make arm holes in the sides.

Cut 4 large circles of felt to cover the balls. Cover them and gather felt at the back of each and stitch. Tack the four balls together in a row. Attach a loop of elastic to the back of the top ball long enough to go round the neck. Attach a second length between the middle two balls to go around the waist, and a similar length to the back of the bottom ball to go around the hips.

Make a green felt balaclava as shown on page 140. Wear over green tights and leotard.
Put on peas, balaclava and pod, then tack or pin pod comfortably to peas at front.

A Circus Tent

Perfect for a pregnant lady – you could be expecting quins inside this costume and no one would be any the wiser. My sister-in-law Wendy looks so elegant in it, and being made with crinoline hoop it's not rigid at all and can easily be squashed either way for manoeuvrability. You could even make a frame for it afterwards and use it as a play house for those quins.

MATERIALS

(To fit anybody!)
5m 70cm white cotton or old sheets
    (or striped material) 115cm wide
6m 40cm tape 2.5cm wide
7m trimming
red fabric or paint for stripes
6.5m crinoline hoop 1.5cm wide
small piece buckram for hat
4 coloured remnants for flags
2 garden sticks
plasticine
remnants for clown

Cut a 3.2m length of white fabric. Either paint with red stripes or cut strips about 6cm wide from the red fabric and stitch these across the width of the cotton at intervals of about 10cm (fig. 1).

Bring ends of striped fabric together, forming cylinder, and place black fabric behind the join. Stitch along top and side edges of black through the striped fabric (fig. 2).

Stitch 25mm wide tape 25mm beneath top edge of this 'skirt', and taking care to leave tent flaps free, stitch tape around bottom edge, leaving 10cm open for threading. Cut a 3.2m length of red fabric, 10cm wide, cutting one edge in decorative loops. Stitch along top straight edge to top of 'skirt' above the tape channel.

For yoke

Cut two pieces of cotton as fig. 3.

Decorate with further strips of red fabric or paint (fig. 4).

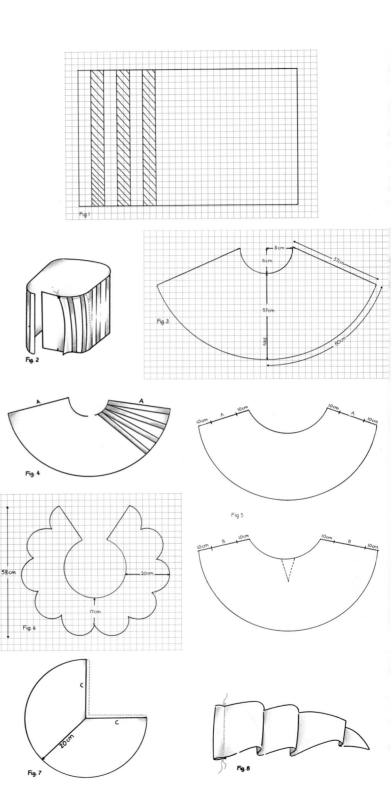

Right sides together stitch edges A to edges B 10cm in from top and bottom forming armholes (fig. 5). Make a 17cm slit at back centre. Cut one piece white cotton as fig. 6. Edge with braid, and stitch to top of yoke at neck edge, matching ends to slit in yoke.

Right sides together, matching sides and centre back and front, sew lower edge of yoke to top edge of 'skirt' above tape channel.

Thread half of crinoline through top tape channel, and half through bottom, overlapping and taping ends. Cut shape in buckram as fig. 7, and cover in white cotton. Edge with braid. Overlap edges C and stab stitch together. Attach elastic on inside to fit under chin.

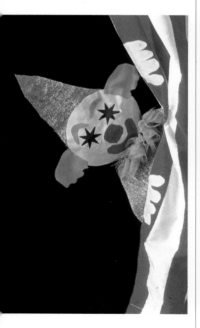

Cut 4 flag shapes in buckram and 2 shapes in each colour scraps to cover them. Zig-zag colour onto both sides of buckram leaving small gap at one corner (fig. 8). Stitch 1.5cm away from straight edge to form channel for stick. Break garden canes in two, and insert into flags. Push 3 flags through small holes made in top rim of tent and tack in position underneath. Push last flag through top of hat and on inside wedge plasticine around stick to secure.

Draw up one tent flap and secure. Applique a little clown from remnants and two hands on flap edge.

83

Fig.1

Fig.2

Fig.3

Fig.4

Fig.5

This could take you a very long time to make – simply because you may have to read through all your old postcards before wanting to cut them up. It's a wonderful use of existing materials, and although you could paint the cards if you liked, I think the pictures give the effect of Japanese lacquer.

Fig.6

Unicorn

A few years ago the Unicorn Theatre organised a procession of little children through London all dressed as unicorns. It was a charming sight. I made this costume for my daughter to wear, and it's still one of my favourites. It would also be lovely to make a junior version of the lion (p. 58) to go with it, giving them a crown to fight over of course.

(p. 58)

MATERIALS

(To fit 4–6 year old)
old coloured postcards (or old
*   greetings cards or coloured card)*
staples
tape for ties
paper fans
hat base – policeman's or bowler
*   novelty hat*
wellingtons
cardboard
silver foil

Cut a postcard in half and staple together lengthwise as fig. 1.

Staple another half postcard over the top of this to make a separate flap (fig. 2).

Make several of these and join together, fanning out slightly as fig. 3. In this way make 1 back and 2 fronts. Shape lower edge with scissors. Join on smaller pieces of postcard round top (fig. 4). Staple on ties.

Staple cards together for front and back of breastplate, cutting out arm and neck holes and adding ties as fig. 5.

Staple shapes of card together to pin onto shoulders, boots, and to hang down front of skirt.

FOR HAT

Cut brim off toy policeman's hat or toy bowler and staple paper fans to sides and back as fig. 6. Cut out fierce shapes from cards and staple onto hat.

Cut a sword from cardboard and cover with foil.

MATERIALS

(To fit 4–6 year old)
two pairs of old white tights
white polo neck jumper
1 mop head
cardboard
staples
gold braid
glue
1 square white felt
elastic
white paint

Cut legs off 1 pair of tights and sew up one hole. Enlarge other hole for face and hem or make white balaclava (see p. 140). Make cone from cardboard, paint white and cover with spiral of gold braid. Cut slits in open end and bend back to form tabs. Attach elastic to go round head (fig. 1).

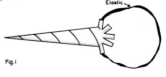

Elastic

Fig.1

Make hole in front of balaclava at forehead. Add two little felt ears. Open out mop head and sew strands along top of balaclava. Bunch up further strands into a tail, and sew onto back of other tights.

Place cone on forehead with elastic going round head. Gently ease balaclava over the head, letting cone project through the hole.

Submarine Commander

uncomplainingly put on the rather less dignified costume I had put together for him.

MATERIALS

*1 white polo neck jumper
2 dish mops
3 gold scouring pads
bits of coloured ribbon, scraps of material
gold buttons or gold milk bottle tops
gold chain and gold braid
3 garden sticks
green fabric remnants
navy blue beret
corrugated cardboard
white scrap of material or crêpe paper
flippers
gold spray
glue
blue paint
plasticine*

Cut strips of card and cover with ribbon pieces or scraps of material to resemble naval decorations. Make a tassel with lengths of gold braid. Sew buttons, 'decorations', chain, tassel and gold braid arm stripes onto jumper.

Spray dish mops gold. When dry, sew to shoulders of jumper. Add a strip of card covered or sprayed with gold and stick it along the handle of each mop. Stick a scouring pad on each. Cut six fish shapes out of green fabric and stitch into three pairs. Make holes and thread onto sticks, gluing if necessary. Cut circle of strong card to fit inside top of beret. Glue in position. Cut a strip of corrugated cardboard to size of wearer's head and glue around bottom edge of beret to form brim. Cut peak out of card, snip at intervals and bend tabs along inside edge and stick to inside of brim. Paint navy blue and trim with gold braid. Cover corrugated brim with white material or paper. Add gold scourer, pushing up front of beret. Make three holes in top of beret and card, push sticks through and secure underneath with plenty of plasticine.

Rodney Bewes knew immediately what he wanted to be when I mentioned the idea of the book to him. He is a very able and keen rower, but obviously dreams of being in charge of a boat somewhat larger. 'I've got a sort of Trevor Howard image in mind' he told me on the 'phone. He was very sporting in the way he

Small Butterfly

I love this costume – it makes such a very pretty outfit in its own right, apart from beautifully giving the feeling of a butterfly. It makes a refreshing change from just sticking a couple of wings onto the back of a leotard: it's very comfortable to wear, and would look marvellous on an adult as well.

MATERIALS

(To fit 8–10 year old)
5.2m white voile 115cm wide
2.4m blue voile 115cm wide
gold, silver, dark blue remnants
wire
black trimming
gold braid
elastic
buckram
30cm zip

Cut 4 pieces, 2 front and 2 back, as fig. 1.

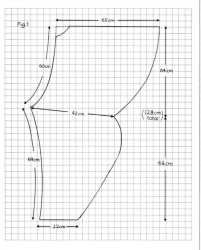

Decorate these pieces before stitching together. Cut out shapes in blue fabric as fig. 2, 4 as top and 4 as bottom, to appliqué onto each of the butterfly pieces. Emphasise solid lines and outline with black trimming.

Cut out 4 shapes as A and 4 shapes as B as fig. 3 in gold.

Stitch into place as shown and edge with gold braid.

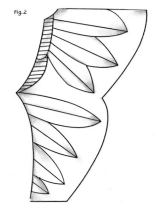

Fig. 2

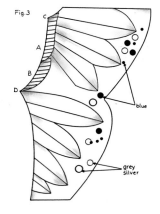

Fig. 3

Cut out large and small circles in silver remnants and dark blue, and stitch into place as shown in fig. 3.

Now stitch centre front and centre back seams C–D, leaving centre back open for 30cm zip. Right sides together, join front to back along shoulders, inside leg seams, and outside seams, leaving 13cm open for arms as fig. 4.

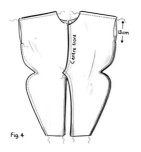

Fig. 4

Elasticate leg holes. Turn right side out.

Cut a strip of buckram about 3cm wide long enough to go around the head. Cover with gold fabric and add a little elastic at the back to join into a circle. Tape or sew two pieces of wire at the front, with a little gold shape stuck on the end of each for the antennae.

Mature Butterfly

Why we always think of butterfly costumes as being for girls I don't know – presumably there must be as many males as females or the butterfly population would be getting a bit thin by now.

I asked my dear friend actor Vernon Smythe if he would wear it for me, and I think he brings great dignity to it. I have known Vernon since working with him when I was about eight years old – I apparently adopted him as an honorary uncle on the spot.

To make this costume needs care and patience. It uses the same method as employed for the giant costumes of the carnivals, but as long as you have the space and can get hold of the cane it is easier to make than it looks.

MATERIALS

(To fit adult)
cane, in as long lengths as possible
polythene
crêpe paper
tissue paper
sellotape
panel pins
spray paint (FEV)
spray glue
magic marker or chalk
masking tape or electrical tape
feathers from feather duster
2 pieces of thin cane or long sticks
old sunglasses
wire and tinsel

Soak cane in bath for an hour or more.

Draw out shape of wing on piece of brown paper or newspaper. Cut out and draw onto wooden floor or back of a flat door, drawing two shapes opposite each other for both wings (fig. 1). Use waterproof magic marker.

Pin damp cane to floor using panel pins. Do not hammer right in, and leave enough sticking out so that the pins can be pulled out with long-nosed pliers when cane is dry.

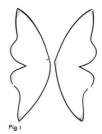

Fig. 1

Follow the outline of the wing, overlapping cane where necessary by a reasonable amount – 8cm or more. Whittle down ends of cane with a stanley knife for smooth joins (fig. 2). (Ignore taping in diagram at this stage.)

Fig. 2

Fill in cross struts – enough to support main outline. When cane is all pinned out leave to dry overnight. Make sure cane is quite dry before removing pins or the tape won't stick. Remove pins bit by bit, taping the cane together tightly as you go. When the last pin is removed and all the pieces of cane are taped together you should be able to lift up the wing without it buckling (fig. 3).

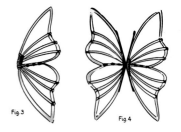

Fig. 3   Fig. 4

Cross brace wings together with two cane struts or metal coathangers (fig. 4). Adjust angle of wings by gently bending cane until the desired angle is reached, holding the cane over the steam of a kettle or over a gas burner to soften, but making sure the steam doesn't take off the tapes. Be gentle as dry cane is brittle.

Pin sheet polythene over front of wings (or you can use net, paper, chiffon – anything light). Fold polythene round to back of the cane and sellotape (or sew if fabric). Try to keep it smooth.

Look at a picture of a real butterfly to get pattern ideas. Spray torn pieces of foil with diluted FEV or coloured inks and with spray glue stick these and other torn pieces of tissue to the backs of the wings.

Tie or sew webbing or wide tape to middle of wings and tie on wearer as for school satchel.

ANTENNAE

Stick some brightly coloured feathers to the tops of the pieces of cane. Attach these onto the sunglasses as shown in fig. 5 by using galvanised wire and tape – the wire can be bent so that the earpiece will still move. Paint the canes or bind with black bias binding and tinsel, sticking more tinsel around the frames of the glasses to make them more insect-like.

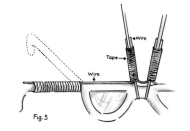

Fig. 5

Wear vest and longjohns in red, and slippers. Stick a few sequins onto all these.

Pencil

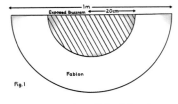

Fig.1

Cut a semicircle of black buckram, 1m diameter, and leaving a

semicircle of 20cm radius uncovered in the centre, cover with wood-look fablon (fig. 1).

Fold into a cone and staple or glue edges together.

About 10cm down from top edge of pencil body, cut armholes. Cut two eyeholes in the black tip. Staple or tape the body part around wearer and position 'hat'.

The charming and talented actor John Gordon Sinclair, star of 'Gregory's Girl', is so tall and thin that he inspired this pencil outfit. It would be fun to wear thickly rubber soled shoes, to represent the rubber on the end, but it's rather a subtle addition. You can just about walk in it, and if you cut eyeholes in the black tip then you can see where you're going. And even if the party you go to is a write-off, at least your costume will have a point.

MATERIALS

(To fit tall adult)
corrugated cardboard, about 1.5m by
*   1.2m, or pieces joined together*
coloured PVC or fablon, to cover
*   cardboard*
1m black buckram
1m wood-look fablon
copydex

Spread cardboard with copydex and cover with the PVC, or stick fablon directly to it.

Spanish Dancer

It's wonderful that you can machine crêpe paper — it means making this sort of thing is very quick and easy. You could equally well do it with lavatory paper like Knickerbocker Glory (p. 40), but of course that doesn't come in such lovely bright colours. I love Martha's stern expression — I told her Spanish dancers always seem to look very serious.

MATERIALS

(To fit 3 year old)
1 packet red crêpe paper
1 packet white crêpe paper
1m cotton or lining fabric 90cm wide
elastic
black leotard

Cut shape from lining fabric as fig. 1.

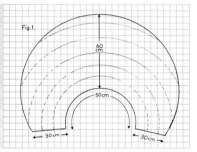

Cut strips of crêpe paper about 7cm wide in the white and about 10cm wide in the red. With one white strip on top of one red strip stitch to main shape, gathering the crêpe into a frill as you go, starting at waist edge, following the curve. Add more frills until the skirt is covered, roughly following dotted lines as shown. Make two extra little frills about 12cm long on pieces of elastic to pin onto shoulders. Put a little elastic at waist if desired and wear over black leotard, pinning or tacking to keep in position.

Tortoise and The Hare

Edward Fox is such a clever and successful actor that his daughter Emilia, much as she obviously adores him, perhaps sometimes dreams of being better at something than he is. I think we all enjoy the story of the Tortoise and the Hare, and it's nice to be allowed to be cheeky to your Dad for once.

MATERIALS

(To fit adult and 9 year old)
For tortoise

corrugated cardboard
green spray paint
50cm beige fabric
2 pairs beige tights
stapler
black felt tip
tape

For Hare

body as for Lion (p. 58) plus 30 cm for
 ears
70cm white fur fabic 115cm wide
2 coat hangers
wadding scrap
60cm buckram

TORTOISE

Cut shape out of corrugated cardboard as fig. 1. Make 15cm long slits all around edge as shown.

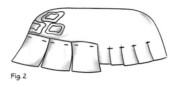

Fig. I

Overlap cut edges and staple to form rounded shell shape. Cut out pieces of cardboard approx. 10cm square and staple around outside. Glue rounded pieces to top of shell, and smaller rounded pieces on top of those (fig. 2). Spray entire shape green.

When dry mark patterns with black felt tip.

Fig. 2

Attach 4 pieces of tape to inside of shell to tie onto body.

Make balaclava out of beige material (see p. 140) and wear tights on arms and legs, letting them wrinkle to resemble loose folds of skin.

HARE

Make body as for Lion (p. 58)

Cut 2 pieces buckram with joins if necessary, 2 pieces brown material and 2 pieces white fur as fig. 1.

Glue buckram to wrong side of each piece of fur fabric. Lay brown fabric pieces on top of buckram and stitch around edge, leaving ends open. Straighten out the coat hangers, twist ends together and make shape as fig. 2.

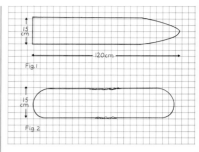

Fig. I

Fig. 2

Slide ears over each end and tack together in middle.

Make balaclava as p. 140

Make two slits on either side of balaclava and push the ear shape through so ears stick out each side. Tack fabric around ears. Tack thick wadding underneath to act as a cushion between wire and head. Bend ears as desired.

Cut fur shape as fig. 3 and tack to chest of body. Cut circle of fur 35cm diameter. Run gathering stitch around edge, pull up and stuff with old tights, newspapers, etc. Tack to back of trousers.

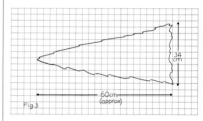

Fig. 3

A Portable Galleon

This is wonderful for a little boy to wear to a party; you could make it into a pirate ship if he liked, or part of the Spanish Armada, or The Golden Hind . . . once you've got the basic shape there are all sorts of imaginative variations. Jo makes a very self-sufficient one man crew.

MATERIALS

(To fit child)
2 cardboard boxes, 1 about 55cm × 30cm × 38cm, 1 about 40cm × 15cm × 26cm
extra cardboard and corrugated cardboard
glue
white paint and coloured spray paints
webbing
masking tape
about 6 green garden sticks
white paper
old doll
chain
1 cardboard tube (from silver foil, etc)
black paint

Cut hole in bottom large enough for hips. Open out all four flaps on top of larger box. Cut front flap as shown, and stick second box onto back flap. Score side flaps as shown, then fold and stick to sides forming long squared off shapes (fig. 1).

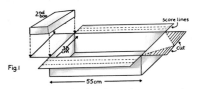

Cut 2 pieces for back and 2 pieces for front as fig. 2. Stick or staple these as shown. Cut piece for deck as fig. 3 and stick to top. Add strip of corrugated cardboard to fit between two front pieces (fig. 3). Stick old doll to this piece for figurehead.

Paint all white, then when dry decorate, using stencil and spray paints. Paint garden sticks in white and allow to dry. Break two or three into varying lengths, then tape to 2 complete ones to form masts as shown (fig. 4).

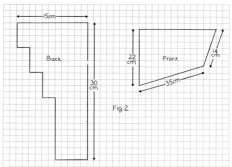

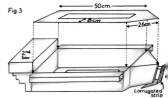

Can-Can Dancer

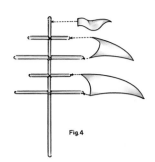

Fig.4

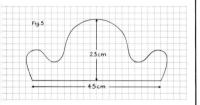

Tape white paper sails onto masts and add a little paper flag to top of each. Makes holes in front and back decks of boat and glue masts in position. Attach webbing straps with staple gun and glue to fit comfortably over shoulders. Add chain and cardboard anchor to back. Cut 2 hat shapes as fig. 5.

Fig.5

23cm

45cm

Cut long strip of corrugated cardboard 90cm × 5cm and staple between two shapes, leaving bottom open. Paint black and red. Add a small mast and sail as for main boat. Make a telescope by sticking a piece of corrugated cardboard round end of cardboard tube, and inserting a smaller roll of corrugated paper into other end (fig. 6). Paint black.

Fig. 6

I had originally intended to string tin cans all over this outfit to really hammer home the point of the joke, but when it came to the photo session, Joanna Lumley looked so beautiful in the crêpe paper dress that it seemed a shame to add any more to it. I just left the two in the hat, which is a far more subtle way of making the pun anyway.

MATERIALS

(To fit size 10)
roll of coloured crêpe paper
roll of white crêpe paper
tape
2 paper plates
about 30cm black and white striped
  fabric 115cm wide
black leotard or bandau top
elastic
cans
bunch of feathers
stapler
wire

Cut circle of coloured crêpe as fig. 1, making joins where necessary.

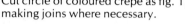

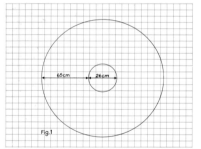

Fig.1

Cut strips of white crêpe about 10cm wide, and stitching down centre of strips, machine around circumference, gathering well as you go (fig. 2).

Fig 2

Turn skirt over, wrong side up, and stitch more strips of white crêpe in the same way in smaller and smaller circles moving into the centre, about 3–4cm apart (fig. 3).

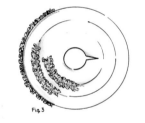

Fig.3

Stitch 2–3cm wide tape to inside of waist edge and fasten with hook and eye.

Cut 2 pieces striped fabric 30cm deep and about 50cm wide. Fold in half lengthways and machine ends to form cylinders. Turn under 1.5cm on upper and lower edges and stitch to form channels for elastic, leaving 3cm open for threading. Thread with elastic (fig. 4).

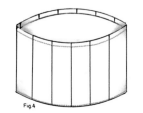

Fig.4

Cut two 5cm wide strips of striped fabric about 50cm wide. With shirring elastic in your machine, or by hand, gather up one strip to fit the neck and the other to fit above the knee, making 4 to 5 rows of stitching.

Make hat base from the 2 paper plates, by folding one in half and stapling behind the other (figs. 5 & 6).

Fig.5

Fig.6

Staple plenty of coloured crêpe onto this base, making flounces at the back and fanning it out around the sides and front, add bunch of feathers. Thread two cans together with wire through holes punched at top and bottom (fig. 7). Attach to front of hat with more wire. Staple narrow elastic on either side to fit under chin.

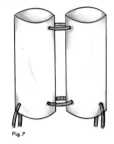

Fig.7

Cut several short strips of coloured and white crêpe, about 5 cm deep, and gather into 2 rosettes, one to be tacked onto the neckband, and one onto the garter (fig. 8).

Fig.8

Milkmaid, Alice, Bo-Peep, Miss Muffet

Katie had to be a milkmaid in a school play a couple of years ago and I made this very sweet dress and apron from Little Vogue 1326 pattern. Rather than not have it worn much afterwards we have adapted it many times since, and these pictures show how, with the aid of a simple prop or two, one outfit can be used for various different costumes – apart from being very pretty just worn on its own as a dress of course. Ashley looks charming in all the variations.

MISS MUFFET:
Rubber spider (or made from wool), dish, spoon, mob cap.

ALICE:
Striped stockings (or draw stripes onto white ones with felt tip), hairband.

MILKMAID:
Mob cap (see Nell Gwynne (p. 118). two little buckets tied onto a garden cane.

BO-PEEP:
Toy sheep, bonnet, mob cap with wide ribbon round, crook (stick with cardboard shaped top and ribbon).

Dr Jekyll and Mr Hyde

A wonderful, fascinating story — and quite chilling, when you consider that Mr Hyde is supposed to be lurking inside all of us. This costume is great fun to make and works very successfully — Paul Jones, having come expecting to be a harmonica, threw himself wholeheartedly into the part, and gamely tried to play a goody and a baddy at the same time, rather like auditioning for a horror film with your right side and a remake of Doctor in the House with your left . . .

MATERIALS

(To fit adult)
waistcoat and trousers from old suit
white coat
white shirt
black tie
bias binding
copydex
powder paints
fake fur bits
20cm flesh coloured remnant
1m black fabric
15cm buckram
hat as Victorian Boy but larger
polythene sheet
lavatory paper
1 rubber glove (right hand)

DR JEKYLL SIDE

Edge waistcoat with black bias binding to give more of a Victorian look. Cut white shirt in half down the back. Save the right sleeve to use as Mr Hyde's arm. Fit shirt behind the waistcoat, tacking up centre back and at shoulder. Mr Hyde's chest will be attached at centre front. Turn up ½ collar and stitch ½ tie in place.

Cut white coat in half and fit the half over shirt and waistcoat, tack down centre back of waistcoat, and to the shoulder seam.

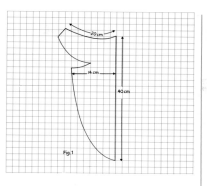

When dry, stitch or glue centre front edge behind the edge of Jekyll's ½ shirt front and collar, and stitch a hook to centre back neck, and an eye to centre back of Jekyll's collar to fasten. The 'half chest' can be tucked behind the waistcoat.

For the face cut a further piece from the remnant to fit over right half of face and front of neck. Build up with copydex and lavatory paper as for chest, making eyebrow and ½ lips etc. Use ½ ping-pong ball painted with false pupil for the eye, and make a small hole next to it to see through. When almost dry, fit on face and pinch into tucks around chin. These will remain stuck as the copydex dries. Attach elastic to go from edge of mask at front hairline, right round head and to join other side of mask above real ear. Glue lower neck edge behind neck band of chest piece.

Cover right hand rubber glove in a similar way. When dry, stitch into the cuff of the right sleeve of the white shirt that you have kept by. Stitch this sleeve into the right armhole of the waistcoat.

For ½ cloak: cut ¼ circle in black fabric as shown in fig. 2. Cut two ½ collar shapes in black and one in buckram. Sandwich buckram between two black pieces, right sides out, and stitch together all around the edge. Stitch inner curved edge of cloak piece to lower edge of ½ collar. Tack to Mr Hyde's neck piece at centre front and to centre seam at back.

MR HYDE

Cut a piece from remnant to fit behind right side of waistcoat as fig. . Copydex, when thickly applied and left to dry will give a clear, rubbery surface like nasty skin. It can also be coloured by mixing with powder paint. Lay the fabric onto polythene sheet and plaster with copydex. Apply strips and lumps of lavatory paper for wrinkles and warts then more copydex, in various colours, into which can be pressed bits of fur. Use hair dryer to speed drying.

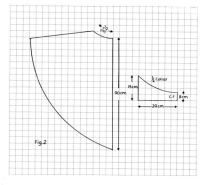

Wear top hat tipped to the Mr Hyde side.

99

Teddy Bear's Picnic

I had great fun sticking this all together and about the best part was picking it up when dry. It felt rather like some sort of conjuring trick.

MATERIALS

1 old tablecloth
paper plates and cups
plastic knives and forks
paper napkins
scraps of foam rubber, wadding,
  remnants
paper cake cases
fur fabric for ears (see Leo p. 58)
plastic headband
copydex
straws

Make cakes from foam rubber – an effective swiss roll can be made by rolling up a rectangle of foam with a little strip of red material each end, stick with copydex and sellotape until dry. Dust with a little flour. Use brown material to look like chocolate icing for other cakes, and some with pink. Make sandwiches from pieces of wadding full of scraps of material. Stick everything onto paper plates and then stick plates, knives and forks, cups, and napkins onto tablecloth. Stick straws into cups.

Cut ear shapes as Leo (p. 58) and stitch into pairs. Stitch to headband.

Pin cloth to shoulders and wear ears.

Minnie Mouse

I made this a few years ago for myself to wear to the Chelsea Arts Club New Year's Eve Ball – not at all the enormously grand and large event it used to be as mentioned in the introduction, but great fun. It was very comfortable to wear, and since the popularity of the ra-ra last year, the skirt length looks really quite fashionable. It would be nice to make a Mickey to go with her.

MATERIALS

(To fit adult, size 10)
90cm green felt 90cm wide
yellow remnant
black remnant
plastic hairband
30cm black buckram
black leotard and tights, yellow shoe

Cut 2 shapes in black buckram as fig 1.

FISHES

Angel Fish

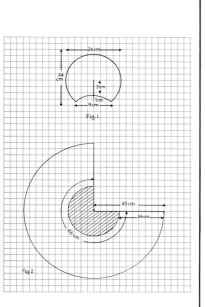

Fig.1

Fig.2

Cut 5cm slit up centre of each, overlap by 2cm and stitch with zig-zag. Stitch by hand to either side of plastic hairband.

Cut three-quarters of a circle from green felt as fig. 2. Cut out hole in centre, radius 11cm for waist. Cut circles from yellow remnant and glue or stitch them on. Sew up back seam, leaving 18cm open. Add hook and eye.

FOR TAIL

Cut narrow strip of black remnant about 80cm long, starting 10cm wide and tapering to a point. Fold in half longways and stitch up edges, leaving top edge open. Turn, lightly stuff open end, sew up and pin or tack to underneath of skirt at back.

When I played Hester in the film 'The Greengage Summer' when I was thirteen years old, I worshipped the young star Susannah York. At my painful stage of adolescence she seemed everything I wanted to be — beautiful, confident and successful. I have never lost my enormous admiration for her, and wanted to think of a costume worthy of someone I had looked up to for so long. I was very pleased with this idea, as it seems to reflect Susannah's combination of English angelic innocence with her glamorous sexiness.

MATERIALS

(To fit size 10)
3m silver fabric 115cm wide
4.4m 'chiffon' 115cm wide
coloured scraps, in greens, blues,
   reds
56cm zip
buckram

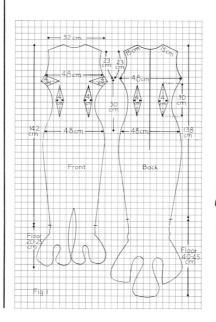

Front   Back

Fig.1

Cut one front and one back in silver fabric (fig. 1).

Make darts as shown in front and back. Right sides together, stitch shoulder and side seams. Cut 56cm slit down centre back for zip. Adjust dress to fit wearer at darts and side seams, as it should hug the figure. Fit zip (as instructed on packet).

Cut 4 shapes in chiffon (fig. 2).

Join into pairs by stitching along edges AB, right sides together.

Open out and decorate each pair with scraps of coloured sparkly chiffon, organza or similar. Right sides together, stitch top seam CD, leaving 32cm open at centre for head. Fold shape along CD right side out and pin front to back around fin shapes leaving open from E to F. With zig-zag stitch, sew around edges from C to E and from D to F.

Cut 2 circles in buckram to fit head, and 2 in silver. Glue 2 buckram pieces together, then glue or stitch silver fabric onto both sides.

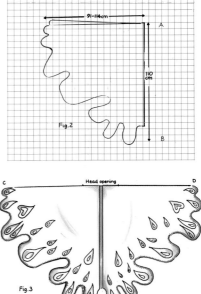

Fig.2

Head opening

Fig.3

Salmon (Smoked or rock!)

Christopher Cazenove, in a velvet smoking jacket, manages to look extremely suave and confident even while wearing a fish on his head, and Paul Jones went spontaneously into some wonderful heavy rock numbers while doing his photographs. A very easy-to-wear, comfortable costume for someone who doesn't fancy a complicated outfit.

MATERIALS

(To fit adult)

2.4m pink lining fabric
1.2m medium weight wadding
scraps for eyes

Cut 4 shapes in pink fabric and 2 in wadding (fig. 1).

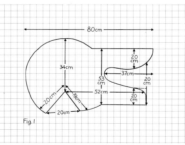

Fig. I

Sandwich each piece of wadding between 2 pink pieces, right sides out, and stitch around outside edge.

Mark gills and scales on outside of each fish shape and stitch through all three layers (fig. 2).

Cut 2 circles 9cm in diameter in white fabric and 2 circles 4cm in diameter in black or dark blue. Glue dark circles into white ones for pupils, then zig-zag eyes into position on head pieces.

Right sides together, stitch head pieces together, leaving open at face and neck. Turn right side out and finish off raw edges.

Add pipe and smoking jacket for Smoked Salmon, or microphone for Rock Salmon.

Fig. 2

Skate

Another nicely silly pun. Jill is wearing my daughter's skates, and from her confident pose you'd think she was quite at ease in them. In fact she couldn't move an inch without falling over, and we had to carry her into position and practically nail her to the floor.

MATERIALS

(To fit adult, size 10–12)
2.4m of 154cm wide beige fabric (or
*   4.8m of 91cm wide)*
2.4m interfacing 91cm wide
scraps for eyes
80cm velcro
glue

Cut two shapes in beige fabric and one in interfacing as fig. 1.

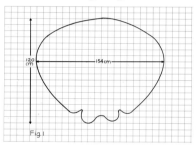

Fig.1

Stitch or iron the interfacing to inside of one shape. Place shapes wrong sides together and stitch around edge, leaving openings for hands (fig. 2).

Stitch through all thicknesses around rough outline of wearer's body and along 'fin' lines (fig. 2).

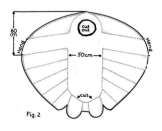

Fig. 2

In the side that's interfaced, cut a head hole and an opening for the legs. Take care not to cut through the second layer of fabric (fig. 2).

Cut a 20cm by 10cm strip of fabric, fold lengthwise and stitch. Attach one end to centre front and the other end to centre back at bottom of the body channel (fig. 3).

Cut two pieces fabric as fig. 4. Stitch together around edge and stuff lightly with old tights, etc. Stitch to lower edge of skate outline (fig. 3).

Down centre back cut opening 75cm long and attach velcro to fasten (fig. 5).

Cut eyes and pupils out of scraps and glue on to back of head.

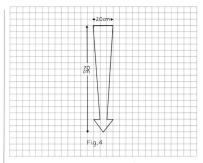

Fig.4

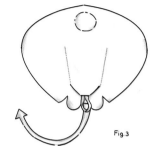

Fig.3

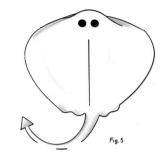

Fig.5

Jelly Fish

This was partly inspired by seeing the wonderful 'Cirque Imaginaire', which Victoria Chaplin and her husband presented in London recently. The umbrellas used in that were specially made of course, and larger and more elaborate than this, but the principle is the same. If the wearer gently opens and shuts the umbrella, beautiful floating effects can be produced.

MATERIALS

1 transparent umbrella
3m bubble pack
remnants of floaty blue and green
    material
stapler

Cover the umbrella with bubble pack, stapling it in pieces to the edge and across the top. Cut long strips from more bubble pack, and staple these and long strips of remnants to the edge.

Red Riding-Hood and her Granny

MATERIALS

(To fit 4–5 year old and an average granny!)

For Red Riding-Hood:

3.6m red fabric 115cm wide
red bias binding
ribbons

For Granny:

80cm white fabric and lace for trimming
blanket

Cut 2 fronts as fig. 1, and 1 back by placing line A–B on fold of material.

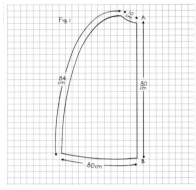

Right sides together stitch up side seams.

Cut 1 hood as fig. 2.

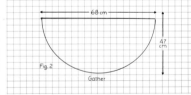

Run around curved edge of hood with long stitch or by hand and pull up to gather until it matches neck edge. Stitch to inside of neck edge and cover raw edge with bias binding. Add ribbons or strips of fabric for ties.

For granny's mob cap see Nell Gwynne (p. 117).

My brother Peter, who lives abroad, says every time he comes home to England he wonders if he'll find a little bent, white-haired old lady opening the door, wearing a mob cap and long white nightie. But as with so many grandmothers nowadays, my mother seems to have boundless energy and to behave and dress just as she always did – and not at all as a story-book granny should. I think our little Red Riding Hood (Sarah, one of her four grandchildren) was quite surprised to see her sitting down!

Robin Hood

Still a very popular character and easy to make – in these days of feminism quite suitable to have it worn by a pretty girl like Pikka. The little jerkin might be fun to wear afterwards with jeans.

MATERIALS

(To fit 8–10 year old)
hat made from 40cm green felt (see p. 140)
1.5m leather-look fabric
garden sticks and card for arrows
feather

Cut 2 fronts and 1 back in leather fabric as fig. 1. Right sides together, sew fronts to back at shoulder and side seams.

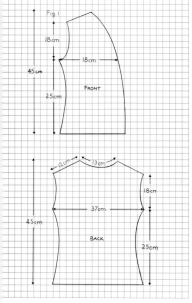

FOR QUIVER

Cut circle in leather fabric 11cm diameter, and a rectangle 35cm by 43cm. Right side in, stitch along long side to form a cylinder, then right sides together, pin and stitch one end to the circle. Turn right side out. Attach long strip of leather fabric to top and bottom. Make arrows from garden sticks with card flights stuck onto ends. Add a feather to the hat.

Wear jerkin over a suitable shirt and tights, and with shoes as for Medieval Boy (see p. 28).

Girl Jumping Out of Cake

(or Sex Object Part Two, see page 79)

MATERIALS

large piece of strong cardboard
corrugated cardboard
2.8m crinoline hoop 1cm wide
wide strong sticky tape
staple gun
white paint
wadding
1 packet green and 1 packet white
crêpe paper
silver doilies
silver foil
glue
stiff paper
pink paint
scraps yellow paper
millinery wire
remnant pink material and scraps red
material
string
braces
2 old stockings or tights
old newspapers etc.

Cut a circle out of the cardboard about 44cm radius. Cut a section out of the back and a hole in the middle large enough for the wearer to slide in sideways and fit in the middle. Cut a piece of corrugated cardboard about 2.5m long and 55cm wide. Stick this cardboard around the edge of the cardboard circle with tape, leaving opening for getting in. Stick length of crinoline hoop around bottom edge in a complete circle to brace the corrugated cardboard – wearer will have to step into this hoop before sliding into cardboard shape (fig. 1).

Paint side white. With staple gun and glue attach wadding strips to top and bottom, gathering to look like puffs of icing. Slash lengths of green and white crêpe paper to look frilly and stick on top of each other around side. Add silver doilies and strip of silver foil.

Roll pieces of stiff paper into cylinders and staple. Paint pink. Bend flame shapes from millinery wire and cover with yellow paper on both sides. Insert into tops of cylinders. Slit bottoms of cylinders and bend to form tabs. Splay these out and glue candles around edge of top (fig. 2).

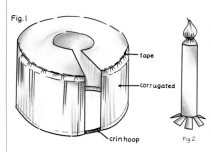

Cut piece of wadding to fit top and stick, slashing centre to look like broken icing and making holes for candles.

Cut two circles from pink remnant about 10cm radius. Stuff 2 old stockings with newspaper etc and coil into bosom shape. Cover with the pink fabric and add a red fabric nipple to each. Attach string at each side and tack 'bosoms' together at centre.

Clip braces to edge of cake between top and side at front and back, adjusting to make the cake balance comfortably. Sling bosoms round neck and add a party hat and sock suspenders.

HALLOWE'EN

I think bats are very charming creatures, although it can be quite unnerving when they flap around your face at dusk. I remember going down the caves at Wookey Hole as a child, and being enthralled by the birds circling around in the semi-dark – once I was told they were bats I was terrified! Poor bats – I don't think they at all deserve their spooky reputation. Still, as long as they have it they make good companions for witches and wizards, especially at Hallowe'en.

MATERIALS

1 papier mâché head shape (p. 140)
1 old umbrella, dark blue or black
black polo neck
black tights
black, pink and white paint

Cut off lower half of head shape as shown, leaving teeth on edge (fig. 1). Cut 2 ear shapes from discarded portion. Paint all black, except for pink muzzle and insides of ears, and white teeth. Glue ears in place. Make two eye holes.

Break off handle of umbrella and slit up to middle from edge. Remove a wedge if necessary. Wear polo neck jumper and pin sides of umbrella to arms, and centre to back of neck.

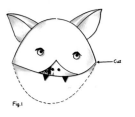

Fig.1

Baby Witch

Damion looks as if he's putting a very fierce spell on us — and with the good fairy turned into a frog (p. 120), who is to save us?

MATERIALS

(To fit 5 year old)
3.8m black fabric 115cm wide
1 cereal packet
raffia
tape
scraps of coloured materials

Cut 2 backs as fig. 1, and 1 front by placing line A–B on fold of material, and following dotted line at neck.

Right sides together, join front to backs at shoulder and side seams, leaving 28cm open for armholes. Cut 2 sleeves as fig. 2.

Sew underarm seam on each sleeve, right side inside. Turn right sides out and stitch into armholes, matching underarm seams to side seams. Make seam at back, leaving opening for head. Add hook and eye.

Cut cape: circle of black material 75cm diameter. Cut hole for head off centre so that cape will dip at back. Cut slit at front (fig. 3).

Flatten out cereal packet and fold into cone shape. Trim bottom and staple. Cover with remains of black fabric. Machine lengths of raffia onto tape and stick to inside of hat.

Stick cut-out stars and moons, etc to dress and cape.

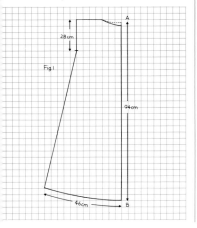

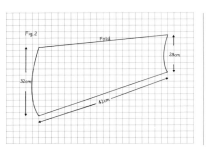

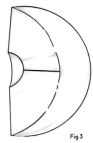

Headless Ghost

This is always very successful at Hallowe'en parties. If you make little hole at the front of the shirt, then you can see out quite easily and keep your identity a secret as long as you like!

MATERIALS

1 white shirt, large, and adapted as
for Charles II (p. 117)
1.2m black cotton 90cm wide, made
into trousers as for Father
Christmas (p. 128) except shorter
and with elastic in bottoms
2 red pan scourers, scraps of gold
paper, elastic
1 papier mâché head shape, or large
sponge beach ball
paints
old hat
1 coat hanger
scraps of wadding
belt

Bend the coat hanger into a long almost rectangular shape, with the hook part bent over in the middle. Tack wadding under the centre to protect the head. Stitch 2 pieces of elastic as shown to go under chin and keep hanger in position. Fig. 1.

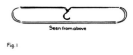

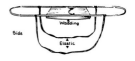

Paint papier mâché head or beach ball to look like head (I found a head off an old model used for a film, but the papier mâché or beach ball will look just as effective). Put old hat on the head and add a feather.

Put together 'rosettes' for shoes as for Charles II (p. 117). Wear hanger on head, place shirt right over the top and pin belt in position to give illusion of waist.

Baby Ghost

Normally one of the problems when wearing a sheet as a ghost is keeping the eyeholes in a position where you can see through them — this way is more satisfactory and looks just as good. You can also make tiny holes under the ghost's hair to grip the sheet to the real hair underneath to stop it slipping.

MATERIALS

(To fit small child)
1.3m white cheesecloth or old sheet 115cm wide
10cm white net 5cm wide
Black felt tip pen

Fold cheesecloth in half lengthwise and trim as necessary so that it will reach the ground when worn. With zig-zag stitch attach 4 layers of net to the front where face will be, then cut away cheesecloth. Make seams up sides, leaving openings for hands (fig. 1).

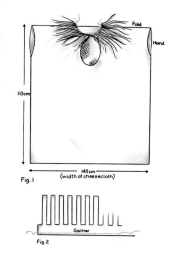

Fig. 1

Fig. 2

Cut strips of remaining net, slash and gather up (fig. 2).

Stitch net hair to cheesecloth as shown in fig. 1.

Draw spooky face onto net with felt pen.

Nightmare

David looks so scary in this that I thought I'd better include a picture of him without his mask in case any young readers find it difficult to sleep tonight!

MATERIALS

(To fit adult)
4m black polyester 152cm wide
papier mâché mask (see p. 140)
scraps of foam rubber or wadding
black paint spray, white paint
broom handle or long stick
cardboard and silverfoil

Cut 2 double shapes as fig. 1 for front and back.
Cut front neck a little lower.

Take pieces A which were cut from between sleeve and skirt, and stitch onto ends of sleeves as shown to elongate them.

Right sides together, match front and back pieces. Stitch top arm seams and underarm and side seams from wrist to hem.

Slash hem and sleeve edges to look ragged.

Cut piece for hood (fig. 2).

Machine up back seam as shown, right sides together. Turn right side out. Gather lower edge into neck opening and stitch.

Slash face edge.

Stitch long strips of remaining fabric around neck and shoulders to give tattered effect.

Make scythe shape in cardboard and cover with silver foil. Tape to broom handle.

Cover mask with pieces of thin foam or thin wadding as shown in fig. 3, cutting holes for eye sockets and nose.

Spray with black paint, then highlight with white.

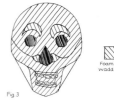

Foam or wadding

Fig. 3

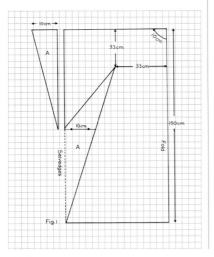

Fig. 1

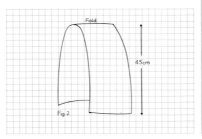

Fold

45cm

Fig. 2

Witch

You must have a witch at Hallowe'en, so here is Doug is a nice scary one. My daughter's frog on the hat makes a very suitable 'familiar' as I believe they call them.

MATERIALS
(To fit adult)

coat as for nightmare
corrugated cardboard
cardboard
wire
red sticky tape
red raffia
foam rubber
black and green spray paints
broom
frog

Cut a large brim from the cardboard, with a hole in the middle to fit head. Cut a piece of corrugated cardboard and bend into a cone shape. Staple. Slit the lower edge and bend up into tabs. Glue these to underneath of brim. Spray black. Glue lengths of raffia 'hair' to inside. Bend glasses shape out of wire and cover with red tape. Cut nose out of foam rubber, including a few warts. Spray green. Glue or tape to glasses. Carry broom and position frog on hat, wiring in place.

Skeleton | A Mummy

This little skeleton looks so charming that it's hard to imagine being frightened by it, but as it may be going to a party where all the guests are of similar age that's probably a good thing – I have known a small hostess reduced to floods of tears at a Hallowe'en party by the arrival of a particularly cleverly dressed monster!

MATERIALS

(To fit 4–6 year old)
1 pair black tights (thick)
1 black polo neck jumper
1 skeleton mask, or make your own
   (p. 114)
white paint, washable
1 black stocking, or half pair of tights

Put the clothes on to the wearer and, if they can bear it, paint in bones as accurately as possible. It feels rather cold and wet but is worth it in the end. Carefully slide off tights and jumper and allow to dry. Wear the stocking over the head with a hole cut for the face and the mask over it.

Another very easy costume – not exactly long-lasting, but it should stay long enough to make a very effective entrance. Don't be tempted to do this with crêpe bandages; it can apparently be quite dangerous if they are wound too tightly. This method given here is 100% safe, fun to do and very cheap.

MATERIALS

white lavatory paper
sellotape

Wind the paper round and round until the whole body is covered, taping as necessary. You'll find it tends to tear along the perforated lines unless it is pulled very gently. When face is covered, very, very carefully make eyeholes.

These two outfits for Charles II and Nell Gwynne are made almost entirely of old curtains. I think they look far better on Gemma Craven and Frazer Hines than they ever did at a window. Charles' waistcoat and shirt are decorated with glue, paper doilies and pasta, and his magnificent wig is just sprayed wadding. From the lascivious look on Frazer's face I think Gemma is going to need all her spare oranges.

MATERIALS

(To fit adult)
Charles II

pair old jeans, preferably white
old white shirt
1 velvet curtain, preferably red
gold-coloured wood glue (p. 140)
gold paper doilies
white paper doilies
gold painted pasta wheels
2 red pan scourers
2 gold pan scourers
80cm thick wadding
old newspaper
black spray paint
small amount red ribbon or red crêpe
blue remnant or blue crêpe for sash
elastic
copydex

Cut off the jeans just below the knees, turn up 3cm on inside of each leg and stitch, leaving opening for threading. Thread with elastic.

Gather up two 20cm lengths of red ribbon or crêpe paper into rosettes and stitch into the centre of each gold scourer. Stitch a scourer to the outside knee of each trouser leg. Decorate outside seams with gold glue and centres cut out of gold doilies.

Cut off part of the collar of the shirt, so that when turned up it makes a straight line. Staple pleated paper doilies one above the other onto the front and around the cuffs.

Stick gold painted pasta wheels at neck and around cuffs.

For waistcoat: Cut 2 shapes from velvet curtain as fig. 1.

Cut 1 shape as fig. 2.

Right side inside, fold and stitch darts in front shoulders. Right sides together, stitch back and fronts together at shoulders and side seams, leaving AB open for armhole. Finish off hem.

Mark button holes up left hand front with gold glue and allow to dry. Add pieces of gold doily to both sides of front and around hem stuck with copydex. Stick gold painted pasta wheels to right hand front for buttons.

Gather up pieces of gold doily and stitch to centres of the 2 red pan scourers. Add narrow elastic to fit round shoes. Make a cummerbund by pleating a length of red ribbon or red crêpe and tack or pin around the waist. Add a length of blue material or paper for a sash.

For the wig: Carefully split the wadding into 2 layers and use wool inside uppermost. Tack two 80cm edges together, then make a deep fold on either side of this seam on the front edge, tapering off like darts. Stuff these two peaks with newspaper and stitch underneath. Trim away wadding around face and shape shoulders. Spray black. (Figs 3 and 4).

MATERIALS

(To fit adult)
Nell Gwynne

2 patterned curtains
2 lace or net curtains
80cm white fabric 115cm wide
shirring elastic
narrow elastic
scrap pink ribbon
corrugated cardboard
1m gold cord
paper ribbon
oranges
2 pedal bin liners, old newspaper

Blouse: Cut a piece of white fabric 92cm × 40cm and stitch up shortest end to form tube.

Cut 2 widths off one of the lace curtains 16cm deep and stitch the ends together, right sides together. Turn under 1.5cm along one edge and stitch to form channel for elastic leaving an opening for threading. Thread with enough narrow elastic to go around shoulders. Stitch this frill along 20cm of front edge of tube and same at back (fig. 1).

Fig 1

For hat: Cut a circle of white fabric 40cm diameter. Cut another width of the lace curtain 10cm deep and stitch around edge, gathering as you go. With shirring elastic in bobbin of your machine stitch 4 rows around edge of fabric to gather. Tack on a pink bow.

For skirt: Stitch the 2 curtains together down the long edge. Pull up the rufflette tape if still attached to fit

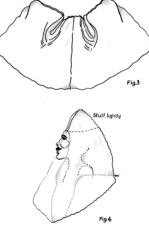

Fig.1   Fig.2

Fig.3

Stuff lightly

Fig.4

waist and secure string. (If not, gather up by hand with strong thread.) Place seam at centre back and join front at top only. Cut a 50cm width of lace curtain, the same length as your curtain skirt. Place behind centre front opening and tack along top edge. Pull curtains back each side to reveal lace and machine half way up. Tack folds of top half in place and decorate with pink bows (fig. 2).

Stuff 2 small bin liners with crumpled newspaper, tie up and stitch under skirt at each side of waist.

Cut piece of corrugated cardboard as fig. 3.

Make holes near short edges, spray black and thread with gold cord to fasten.

Make two bunches of ringlets by curling lengths of paper ribbon with the edge of a sharp knife and staple to either side of mob cap. Staple a few stray curls at front for fringe.

Fit two oranges into bra, poking out of blouse.

Quick Zip-up Mermaid

As soon as I saw a sample of this beautiful material I knew we must make something fishy, and this very simple mermaid is the result. I wanted it to combine the tight, slinky look of the aptly named 'fishtail' dresses of the fifties with the freedom needed for musical bumps, disco dancing and so on. A zip seemed the perfect solution; done up it allows just enough movement for gentle walking, and once the grand entrance has been made it can be unzipped as much as required.

MATERIALS
(To fit 8 year old)

*2.3m of 91cm wide fishy looking
   material
2 scallop shells
silver spray paint
1.5m of flesh coloured elastic
61cm open ended zip
Alice band or old hat
small quantity of green material
elastoplast
pearls, shells etc
glue*

Fold material in half lengthwise and
cut three pieces (fig. 1).

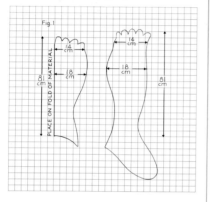

Machine front to back pieces right
sides together, at edges A to edges B.
Set zip between notches in backseam
C (fig. 2).

Fold elastoplast round edges of shells
and then spray with silver paint. Sew
through plastered edges onto strip of
elastic. Attach two further strips of
elastic to top of shells then take over
the shoulders to meet chest elastic at
back. Sew. Attach a small piece of
elastic between shells at centre front.
Sew hook and eye at back (fig. 3).

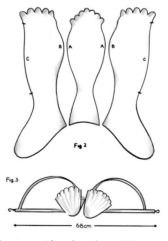

Cover an Alice band or old hat with
green material and decorate with
glued-on pearls, shells etc. and with
long strips of seaweed-like material.

A very simple, easily made tutu
worn over a sleeveless leotard
plus a little trimming makes a
very effective fairy. The top frill
only needs to be very lightly
tacked to the shoulder straps, and
the skirt is entirely separate so
you can use an existing leotard
without having to appear at the
next ballet class looking as if
you've just come off the top of the
Christmas tree! I made the wands
by covering garden canes with
gold sticky tape and adding a star
and a little surplus net, and the
wobbly stars attached to
headbands that were a craze
imported from America last year
make very good antennae. How
sad that Kimberly gets turned
into a frog.

MATERIALS
(will adjust to most children's sizes)

*For each fairy:
1.6m of decorated net
4m of plain net
70cm of 5cm wide belt elastic*

Bad Fairies

Cut a further eight pieces of plain net but this time only 22cm wide. Make two long strips in the same way.

Roughly pin and gather the decorated net to the edge of the belt elastic then machine with zig-zag stitch, stretching the elastic as you go (fig. 2).

Fig. 2

Repeat with the four strips of plain net, ending with the two shallower pieces.

Sew ends of the elastic together to form a circle. This completes your tutu.

From remaining decorated net cut two 10cm strips, join end to end and gather onto the narrow elastic with zig-zag stitch. Attach to top of leotard.

Cut wings shape out of remaining net and attach to back of tutu. Any remnants can be used to decorate hair and wand.

1 sleeveless leotard
1m of 1cm elastic
head decorations and wands

Cut four pieces of decorated net as fig. 1, and join end to end to form a long strip.

Cut eight pieces of plain net in the same way, again 25cm wide. Join four of them end to end to make a long strip. Join the other four similarly to make a separate strip.

Fig. 1

90cm

25 cm

A Pair of the Same Suit

Alan Price and Jill Townsend make a very smart suit – and no doubt as to who wears the trousers. I think it looks very funny to wear to a party, and as this one was made out of old curtains it cost almost nothing.

MATERIALS

(To fit two adults)
4 or 5 old curtains, or 8.70m of fabric 137cm wide
buckram
cardboard
1.30m crinoline hoop 1.5cm wide
tape
scrap for handkerchief
small amount crêpe paper or tissue
corrugated cardboard
remnant white fabric or old sheeting
remnant for tie
glue

FOR TROUSERS

Cut 4 pieces as fig. 1. Cut also false fly and four little strips for belt loops. Make darts as dotted lines. Take two pieces and sew together down length of crutch. Do same to other two pieces.

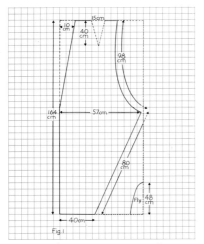

Fig.1

Now you have two pieces. Take one piece and sew the false fly onto the centre front seam, 5cm from top. Sew two of the belt loops onto the front, then sew the other two onto the back piece of the trousers.

Fig.2

Right sides together, sew the two pieces together along inside and outside leg. Turn down 5cm at waist to form channel for crinoline hoop, leaving opening for threading. Thread with crin, overlap and tape.

Sew two lengths of tape to the front and back, crossing over so that they will go over the wearer's shoulders to support the trousers (fig. 2).

Turn up the bottoms to form 6cm turn ups.

Cut a belt from buckram or card, about 1.50m by 5cm. Cut out a buckle and paint belt and buckle brown.

FOR JACKET

Cut one back and two fronts as fig. 3. Sew a double strip of fabric 3cm deep onto left front to look like edge of top pocket. Right sides together, sew jacket together along shoulder and side seams, leaving armholes open.

Cut 2 back collar shapes and 4 lapels as fig. 3.

Right sides together, stitch two back collar pieces together leaving open. Turn and press. Stitch lapel pieces into pairs right sides together from B–B. Turn and press. Stitch lapels to each end of back collar, matching points A. With right side of collar to wrong side of jacket, matching centre backs, stitch raw edge of lapels and collar to raw edge of jacket (fig. 4).

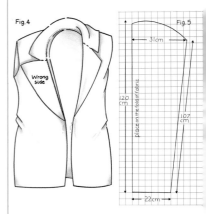

Fig.4   Fig.5

Turn to right side and clip 1cm at bottom of lapels, turn 1cm edge to inside and finish off.

Wrap left side of jacket 10cm over right side and tack invisibly.

Cut two sleeves as fig. 5. Right sides inside, sew underarm seams on sleeves and hem the ends. Matching underarm seams to side seams of jacket, and centre top of sleeves to shoulder seams, sew sleeves into armholes, right sides together.

Fig.3

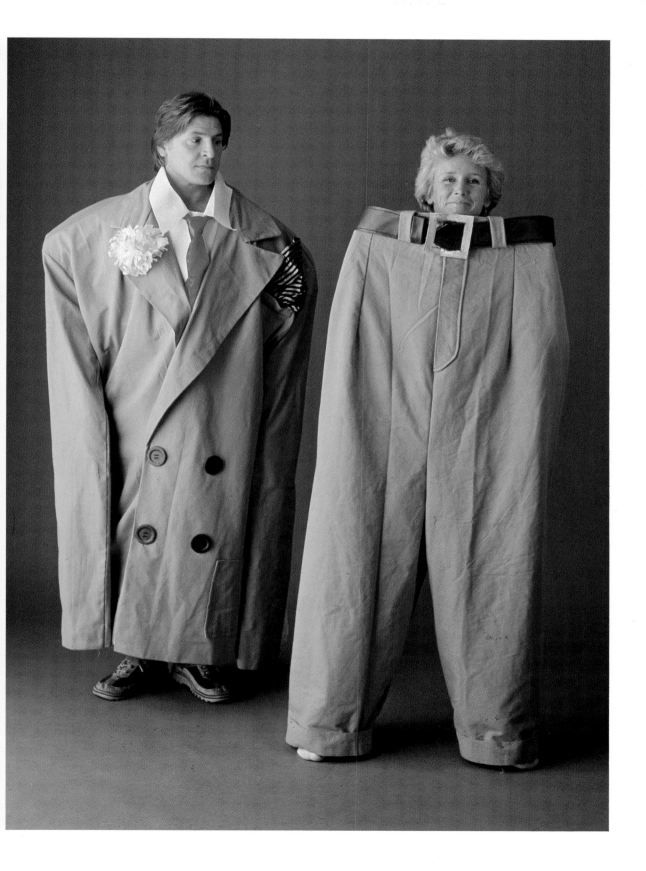

Judge

From some of his sinister performances you would never guess that Donald Pleasence is such a charming, funny and friendly man. I worked with him in a film called 'Henry VIII and his Six Wives', and ever since have been a fan not just of his acting but of him as a person. He was rushing off to Mexico to make a film when I caught him to wear a costume for me – and in spite of sporting a pile of lavatory rolls on his head, a more terrifying judge it would be hard to find.

MATERIALS

lavatory rolls
white paint
strong thread
red blanket
strip of white paper or fabric

Simply thread the rolls together as in fig. 1. Make one long strip to go from forehead over head and down back, and four more to go down sides. Join together with more thread and paint them all white. Wear the red blanket and tie the strip of white paper or fabric round the neck.

Fig.1

Cut 4 buttons from card, paint brown and make 4 holes in each. Stitch to front of jacket. Gather a scrap of brightly coloured fabric along one edge and stitch inside 'top pocket'. Cut some strips of crêpe paper, slash along one edge and gather up along opposite edge to form carnation. Stitch onto lapel.

FOR FALSE SHIRT

Cut a circle of corrugated cardboard 45cm radius. Cut a hole in the middle just large enough to fit over the head. Cut a piece of card or buckram long enough to go round the edge of neck hole and about 14cm deep. Shape ends as shown (fig. 6).

Cut V shapes out of lower edge as

Fig.6

shown and glue to inside of hole in corrugated cardboard. Cut a piece of white fabric and glue it onto cardboard where it will show under jacket. Cut a long strip of material for a tie.

To wear, place corrugated cardboard over the head and allow front and back to flop. Put jacket on over the head and allow the shoulders to rest on the corrugated cardboard.

Step into trousers and fit 'braces' comfortably over shoulders.

CHRISTMAS

This costume not only looks very festive and seasonal – I think it makes a beautiful dress in its own right; it is also another good costume for someone pregnant. For the photograph I wired up some Christmas tree lights to make it extra sparkly, but to wear to a party decorations alone would be fine. I couldn't have had a better person to wear it than Therese Sorrell, who because of her statuesque height was the inspiration for not only this tree but also the Palm Tree (p. 22). Before she married and started a family, Therese was a top model, and it certainly showed in everything she wore for me – I have a feeling she could wear a rubbish bag and make it look like a Paris original.

MATERIALS

(To fit tall adult, size 10)
4.5m green felt 90cm wide
14m 1.50m wide green net
30cm buckram
6m 25mm wide tape
3 lengths of 1.5cm crinoline hoop,
2.90m, 1.90m and 1.50m
ornaments and tinsel
strong sticky tape

Cut three pieces in felt as fig. 1.

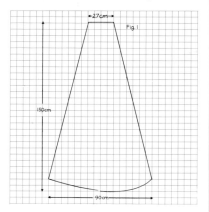

Sew together down sides to form a cone. Lay cone flat, with one seam at centre back. Cut arm holes and neck.

Leave shoulders open at present. Sew three pieces of tape to inside of cone at hem, 70cm up and 40cm up to form channels for hoops, leaving a few cm open for threading (fig. 2).

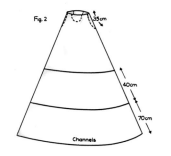

Leaving net double, as it is normally sold, slit a long fold then cut into three 25cm wide strips. Mark guidelines in chalk on the cone, 23cm apart and 18cm apart as fig. 3. Keeping the net double sew it along the middle to each marked ring gathering into a frill as you go, and cutting on completion of each ring (fig. 4).

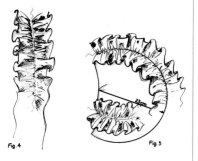

Sew shoulder seams and stitch a frill of net round collar in the same way as before.

Thread hoops into channels, overlap and tape.

Cut a semicircle of buckram, 23cm radius. Cover with felt, stitching around edge. Cut two double lengths of 10cm wide net, 2m long and 1.50m long. Sew to hat shape in same way as on dress, one at edge and one 10cm above (fig. 5).

Join edges to form cone by handstitching. Fit elastic round chin. Decorate tree by sewing or safety-pinning ornaments and tinsel to net and wiring foil covered cardboard star to hat.

Cheap and Cheerful Father Christmas

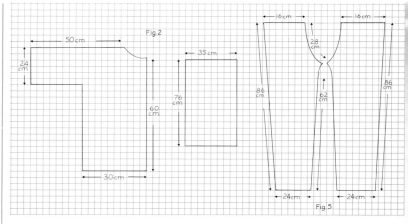

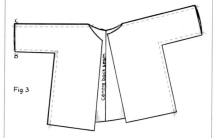

So many people like to dress up as Father Christmas (perhaps just in case the real one doesn't turn up one year?) that I thought it would be a good idea to make one as cheaply and simply as possible. I have used a wincyette fabric which comes in a lovely bright red, is reversible and hardly frays. This saves a great deal of time and trouble. It's trimmed with strips of wadding which again need no finishing off, and both these materials are very inexpensive. The pattern is very simple, the top being based on a T-shape and the trousers on a rectangle, and however basic your sewing skills it really is easy to make.

MATERIALS
(To fit 8 year old)

3m red wincyette 115cm wide
40cm medium weight wadding
61cm elastic
wellingtons, belt, sack
wire

THE JACKET

Cut four pieces as shown in fig. 1.

Cut one piece as fig. 2.

Machine two jacket pieces together at centre back seam. Machine under arm seams B from wrist to hem, and top arm seam C from wrist to neck (fig. 3).

Fold hoodpiece in half lengthwise and then machine along line D, forming neck edge E (fig. 4).

Pin hood onto jacket at edges E, gathering as you go, then machine. Cut strips of wadding 10cm wide and machine round edges of jacket, hood and sleeves.

THE TROUSERS

Cut four pieces as shown in fig. 5.

Stitch trouser legs into pairs as fig. 6

then machine the two pieces together along crutch seam (fig. 7).

Turn in 2.5cm at edge D and machine to form channel, leaving 5cm open. Thread in elastic to fit waist.

Cut a combined moustache and beard shape out of wadding and glue two pieces of wire to the edges for hooking over ears.

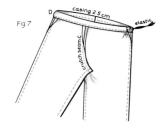

A Christmas Pudding

You may not find any sixpences inside this pudding but I think little Sarah makes it look good enough to eat. Any dark tweedy fabric will give the right impression, and once made it can always double up as a Victorian skirt for an older child (see p. 35). The crinoline underneath can be re-used on its own of course, and could inspire many different costumes.

MATERIALS
(To fit 5–6 year old)

10.8m webbing
1m lining (I used wincyette – cheaper than most lining fabrics) 152cm wide
four pieces of 1cm crinoline hoop, 1.05m, 1.65m, 2.45m and 3.10m
3.10m suitable tweed 115cm wide
1m white 'cream' fabric 90cm wide
small quantity of green shiny lining fabric for holly
6 small red Christmas tree balls
1 plastic headband
wire and fusewire
narrow tape for threading
sticky tape

Cut 12 lengths of webbing 42cm long, a further 12 lengths of 29cm, and 12 lengths of 19cm.

Cut a rectangle of lining fabric 1m by 21cm. Machine short edges together and turn over 25.4mm at top and 25.4mm at bottom to form channels. Make two slits 76mm apart in the outside of both these channels.

Thread tape through slits in top channel. Thread shortest length of crinoline through slits in bottom channel, overlap ends by 5cm and tape. Stitch the twelve shortest pieces of webbing to this hoop at regular intervals (fig. 1).

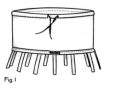

Fig. 1

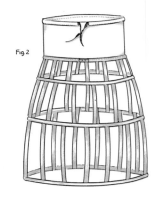

Fig. 2

Form the remaining three hoops by overlapping and taping the lengths of crinoline. Attach the hoops together in ascending size with the pieces of webbing regularly spaced, stitching ends of webbing around hoops (fig. 2).

Cut five pieces of tweed as fig. 3.

Machine tweed pieces together to form pudding basin shape, leaving 10cm unsewn at top of last seam for neck opening. Place over crinoline and sew bottom edge around lowest hoop. Attach hook and eye at neck.

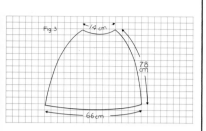

Fig. 3

74 cm

78 cm

66 cm

Cut white 'cream' as shown in fig 4 and drape around shoulders, slipstitching at neck. Make slits in tweed for armholes.

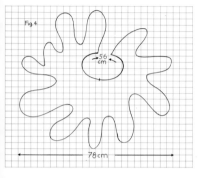

Fig. 4

56 cm

78 cm

Cut 8 large holly leaves out of lining fabric and glue into pairs with wire in centre of each (fig. 5).

Wind ends of wire around headband. Wind fusewire around balls and wire into position.

Fig. 5

Christmas Cracker

I'm sure one would have to put up with all sorts of jokes about being pulled if one wore this to a party – although Therese looks so cool and beautiful that I'm not sure anyone would dare to be so vulgar. As with the other costumes she has modelled for me she manages to make it look more like a Paris gown than some pieces of cardboard and crêpe paper.

MATERIALS

(To fit tall adult)
corrugated cardboard
2.2m crinoline hoop 1cm wide
3 packets red crêpe paper
silver paper doilies
6m red net 150cm wide
narrow elastic
2 lengths of webbing, each 60cm
parcel tape
holly leaves (see Christmas Pudding)
baubles and silver foil

Cut a length of cardboard to fit closely around the body, stapling widths together if necessary. Allow 5–10cm for overlap.

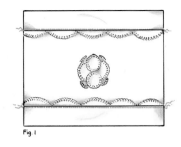

Fig. 1

Elastic

A

Crepe

Net

Fig. 2

Glue strips of red crêpe across its width, leaving most of the top and bottom strips projecting over top and bottom of cardboard (fig. 1).

Decorate centre section with silver doilies and along top and bottom edges of cardboard (fig. 1).

Cut 2 lengths of crinoline hoop to fit the cardboard. Turn cracker shape upright and tape a length of crinoline hoop to inside of top and bottom.

For the net frills: Cut 2 lengths of net, 3m each, which will be double as it is sold. Cut 2 lengths of red crêpe, 3m each. Stitch each length of crêpe to a length of net, placing their long edges flush and stitching close to that edge with a long stitch. Gather up. Cut 1 length of elastic to fit round neck, and one to fit round knees. Zig-zag the edge of each frill, crêpe side out to each piece of elastic (fig. 2). Join the ends of each frill together to make complete circles, sewing through crêpe, net and elastic, but leaving about 20cm open in neck frill to go over head. Attach hook and eye.

Decorate centre of cracker with holly and baubles.

Wrap cracker around body and arms and cut holes just below the upper crinoline hoop for arms. Tape lengths of webbing to inside of cracker to go from front to back over shoulders for support. Tuck the projecting crêpe at top and bottom into the frills.

A Jolly Snowman

This cheap wadding looks remarkably like snow: it's one of the most versatile materials I've used in the book. I made the stones by wrapping scraps of black material round scrunched up silver foil, but I suppose you could use real ones if they weren't too heavy. I didn't have a top hat, but this 50p plastic one gives the right idea.

MATERIALS
(To fit 6 year old)

2.5m medium weight wadding
1.6m white wincyette
2 lengths of 10mm crin hoop, 1.65m and 1.3m
1m tape
'stones'
scarf, hat and pipe

Cut one piece in wincyette and one piece in wadding as fig. 1.

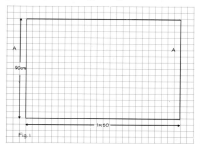

Cut two pieces in wadding only as fig. 2

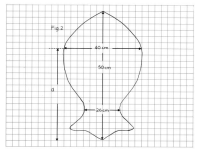

Cut two pieces for balaclava in wadding (see p. 140).

Join edges A of wincyette forming cylinder of fabric. Turn up one 25mm at bottom edge B and machine to form channel for bottom hoop. Sew tape to inside half way up to form second channel C. Turn over 25mm at top edge D to form third channel for gathering (fig. 3).

Make slit in top channel and thread tape through ready for gathering. Make two slits 75mm apart in each of the other two channels and thread with crin hoop starting with lower channel and longer piece of crin, overlapping 5cm and taping together on outside between slits (fig. 4).

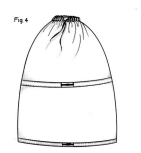

Put shape onto the child, gathering at neck. Wrap wadding around the shape and slip stitch around the bottom edge and at centre front. Tack to neck edge, releasing gathering as necessary. Cut holes for arms. Slipstitch both underarm seams of sleeves marked 'd' on fig. 2, then slipstitch sleeves over armholes taking top of sleeve almost to neck edge. Either leave bottom of sleeve open or slipstitch together, making slit at wrist to allow hands out for eating etc (as in a babygrow). Sew head pieces together.

Tuck headpiece into neck edge. Glue or stitch 'stones' in position. Add hat, scarf and pipe.

Last Minute Jokes

FIRST CLASS MALE

James Coburn, of whom I have always been a great fan, was visiting our house to do some work with my husband Gerald, and was so charming and friendly that he allowed himself to be persuaded into wearing two costumes for me. I certainly couldn't have wished for a better model for First Class Male.

MATERIALS

cardboard
paint
string

Cut a large stamp shape out of cardboard. Copying a real one, paint a stamp design on it – at whatever the current first class rate happens to be. Make holes in the top and thread with string to go around the neck.

THE KING AND I

Just a mere hint of what could be done with film, book or play titles – the possibilities are endless, and often only require the simplest of props.

Simply wear child's or adult's crown, and hang large painted cardboard eye around neck.

VIDEO PIRATE

I love this silly illustration of a modern phrase – it's always pleasing to do something up to date, and there must be many simple costumes to be produced with the aid of a few props. Bryan certainly threw himself wholeheartedly into the swashbuckling role of a pirate.

Simply find some suitably 'piratical' looking clothes, tie a piece of material round the head, make a cardboard eye patch and cram video tapes wherever possible. The sword is a nice touch too if you can get hold of one, if not make one out of foil-covered card.

MATERIALS

cardboard
glue
silver foil

Simply cut a wide belt shape out of cardboard, cover with silver foil and staple around the waist.

HISTORICAL LAUGHTER

My brother-in-law Gordon has worn some very inventive outfits to parties. I remember one time he was intending to go as a Samurai. He put on a kimono and tied a sash around his forehead. Somehow the effect was far too un-warrior like, so he dashed off and found a bicycle wheel, attached it to the end of a scarf which he wound around his neck and reappeared announcing that he was now Isadora Duncan! A little macabre perhaps but certainly unusual . . .

CAPTAIN COOK

Wear a chef's hat and apron, over shirt and waistcoat as for Charles II (p. 117), adding a sail (see Galleon, p. 94) to the hat. Add little saucepan for medals, and carry a telescope (see Galleon, p. 94), and sword. Wear rosettes on shoes as for Charles II (p. 117).

STEEL BAND

When I asked my good friend Paul Jones if he would allow me to photograph him in a costume for the book, he very kindly agreed immediately. 'I should like to be a harmonica,' he suggested helpfully. Well I really did try – I made a cardboard one, a rather natty one out of boxes and plastic bottles, a more symbolic one from foam rubber and silver foil and finally decided that none of them were working. I felt I must indulge his penchant for representing a musical instrument, and so to make up for his losing the one he wanted to be, made him into not just one but a whole band. In name anyway . . . I'm glad to say he wistfully accepted the substitution and posed wonderfully as a steel band.

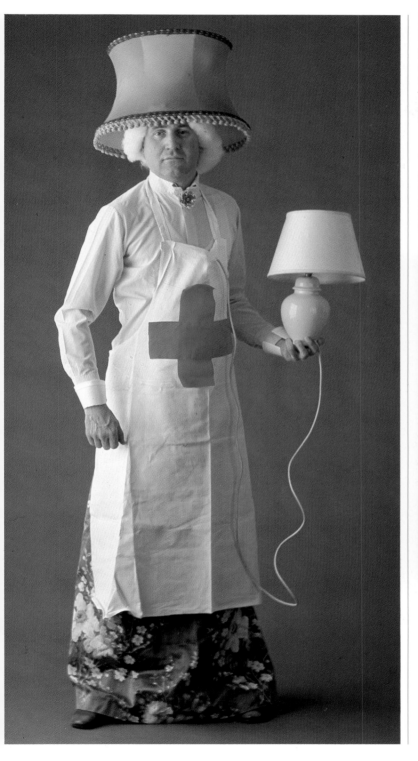

FLORENCE NIGHTINGALE (THE LADY OF THE LAMP)

Shirt with collar turned up and paper cups for cuffs. White apron with large red crêpe paper cross attached. Skirt – old curtain tied round. Wig from piece of wadding. Large lampshade on head, and lamp in hand.

ALEXANDER THE GRATE (*sic*)

Clothes as for Greek Girl (p. 27). Crown from cardboard and fake ermine (wadding marked with felt tip). Sandals. Carry fire irons. 'Soot (burnt cork) on face and arms.

137

PLATO

Clothes as for Greek Girl (p. 27).
Beard from strip of wadding.
Headband as for Greek Boy (p. 27).
Sandals, and carry two plates.

THE DUKE OF WELLINGTON
(THE IRON DUKE)

Shirt and waistcoat as Charles II
(p. 117), plus belt and sword. Wear
wellingtons. Hat (see p. 140).
Carry iron.

HALF NELSON

Hat as p. 140. Wig from strip of
wadding positioned beneath hat.
Shirt as for Charles II (p. 117) with
arm pulled out of one sleeve and
sleeve pinned across chest.
Eyepatch. Telescope (see Galleon,
p. 94). Bottom half should be
ordinary clothes so that one is
only half Nelson.

The Last Straw

James Fox's wife Mary had this
marvellous idea for a very simple
costume. Just stick a straw in your
pocket and carry it off as beautifully
as James does.

Papier Mâché Head Shapes

If you use glue and water instead of flour and water paste, you will get a much stronger papier mâché. You can also use wallpaper paste.

Mix wood glue (PVA) with water until it is of a milky consistency. Blow up a balloon to the size of the head that will wear the head piece. Tear up bits of newspaper and after soaking them thoroughly in the glue mixture, apply them to the balloon, covering the area that you wish to have as your shape. For most of the uses in this book you will need to cover the top half of the back of the head as well as the face area (fig. 1).

When you have one good layer, let it dry. Apply four or five more layers,

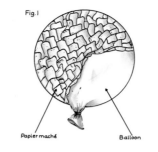

Fig. I

Papier mâché   Balloon

letting each one dry before applying the next. When it is thoroughly dry remove the balloon, bursting it if necessary. The shape will be very hard, and you can now cut it as desired and paint it.

Gold Glue

To make the gold coloured wood glue as used in Queen Elizabeth I, Shorter Oxford Dictionary, etc, simply mix ordinary wood glue (Evostick makes some in a large green bottle) with gold powder. Squeeze it from the tube – or you could use a forcing bag – into the patterns desired. When the glue dries it goes transparent, and you are left with purely gold decorations. If you want to make pearls colour the glue with white powder paint, and so on.

Hats

FOR ROBIN HOOD, PIED PIPER
(Also useful for pixies etc)

Cut 2 as fig. 1 and stitch together two top edges. Fold as shown.
Measurements given fit child about 8 years old.

BALACLAVA
(As for flowers, caterpillar, hare, lion etc)

Cut 2 as fig. 2. Make darts as shown then stitch together around outside, leaving front and neck open. Add fastening at front or stitch.
Measurements are for adult, figures in brackets are for child about 8 years old.

FOR DUKE OF WELLINGTON

(Also useful for other characters)

Cut 1 underneath and two sides as fig. 3 in cardboard. Slash underneath and fold back to fit head. Staple lower edges of side pieces to outer edge of underneath piece. Paint black, and when dry add a little gold braid trimming. Fold white crêpe paper fan wise and cut large feather shapes. Spread out a little and stick to top of hat.

FOR NELSON

(Also useful for other characters)

Take an old soft hat and pin up sides as shown (fig. 4). Paint black and when dry add gold braid trimming.

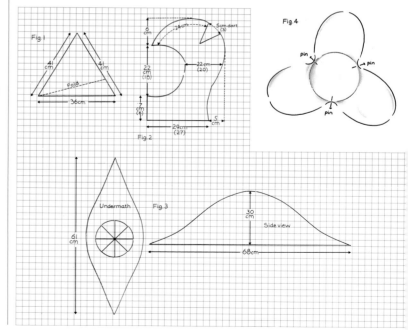

Useful Addresses

JOHN LEWIS AND BRANCHES

Use my local branch of this excellent store, which is
Peter Jones, Sloane Square, London, SW1 (730-3434),
and from there I got most of my fabrics and haberdashery
goods. They have some very good inexpensive fabrics,
two of my favourite discoveries being a very wide
polyester jersey that comes in many colours and which
proved very useful (see Greek couple, Palm Tree,
Caterpillar, etc) and their wincyette, which again is very
reasonably priced and although intended for pyjamas,
makes some marvellous costumes. They have a very good
selection of lining fabrics, which I advise you to use
whenever you want a satiny looking finish. From this type
of shop you will also get rigilene, wadding, interfacing,
and so on. Also look out for good remnants.

BOROVICKS FABRICS
16 Berwick St., London W1 (437-2180)

If you like glittery and unusual fabrics then you must pay
this shop a visit. It is much patronised by theatrical
designers, and when you walk in it almost feels like
entering Aladdin's cave. There I found the beautiful shiny
fishy fabric that I used for the Mermaid, Dragon and
Pisces, and all the gold, silver and glittery bits and pieces,
including the Angel Fish wings, came from there. Do go
and look around.

BY THE YARD FABRICS
14 Berwick St., London W1 (434-2389)

Next to Borovicks and very good value for fabrics,
including nets, linings, etc.

McCULLOCH AND WALLIS
25 Dering St., London W1 (629-0311)

Another very good shop to explore for fabrics and also for
haberdashery including crinoline hoop etc at reasonable
prices.

ELLS AND FARRIER
Princes St., London W1 (629-9964)

Every type of bead, jewel, pearl, and trimming that you
can imagine – just be warned, it is hard to resist if you
have the same taste in glitter that I have. They do a very
good catalogue with samples of all their goods, from
which you can then order by post.

THE BEAD SHOP
Neal St., Covent Garden, London WC1

Also very good for beads etc.

THE BUTTON BOX
44 Bedford St., Covent Garden, London WC1 (240-2716)

Every sort of button you could wish to find.

BRODIE AND MIDDLETON
68 Drury Lane, London WC2 (836-3289)

Gold and silver powders, french enamel varnish (FEV),
paints, etc.

THEATRE LAND
14 Soho St., London W1 (437-2245)

Fabrics, sequins, etc.

THEATRE ZOO
28 New Row, London WC2 (836-3150)

Masks, make-up, glittery hairsprays, etc.

DENNY'S
39 Old Compton St., London W1 (437-1654)

Overalls, white coats, etc, as for Dr Jekyll, Captain Cook
and so on.

BARNUMS
67 Hammersmith Rd., London W14 (602-1211)

Novelty hats, masks, streamers, party presents and
wonderful decorations.

DRAYTON PAPER WORKS LTD.
Sulivan Rd., London SW6 (736-2341)

This is where I got my very wide corrugated cardboard
and my bubble pack. I did have to buy it in large
quantities, so that you may be better off to buy small
pieces and join them together, unless you can team up
with some friends who are also keen craft and hobby fans.
Also try your local yellow pages for paperworks or
packaging material manufacturers near you.

PAPERCHASE
213 Tottenham Ct. Rd., London W1 (580-8496)
and 167 Fulham Rd., London SW3 (589-7873)

A real treasure house – very good for anything made from
paper, and for cardboard, spray paints, felt tips of every
kind and so on. You can also buy bubble pack here in
small quantities, and wonderful gold, silver and
multi-coloured foils.

W. H. SMITH

Very good for stationery goods – they have a marvellous
selection of colours in thin crêpe paper for instance, and
here you can get the powder paints for mixing with the
wood glue (see p. 140).

DEBENHAMS AND BRANCHES

Excellent for fabrics, haberdashery, etc.

HARRODS
Brompton Rd., London SW1 (730-1234)

Well of course Harrods is one of the most amazing shops in the world, and worth a visit whenever you are in the area. Here you will find almost anything you need, and if they don't have it they will order it for you. Don't be tempted to take home a puppy or kitten from the wonderful pets department . . .

LIBERTY'S
Regent St., London W1 (734-1234)

I don't think you would ever regret spending money on a Liberty fabric – they are really beautiful, and the designs are timeless enough to never look out of date. Even the building itself is a work of art. Do go and browse among the wonderful selection of materials.

HOUSE OF FRASER STORES

Very good for a wide range of fabrics, haberdashery, ironmongery, etc.

JUMBLE SALES, OXFAM SHOPS, BRING AND BUY SALES ETC

You can pick up old suits, curtains, hats, etc very cheaply if you keep your eyes open. Also good for junk jewellery to dress up your costumes.

And get in the habit of hoarding cardboard boxes, tubes, yoghurt cartons, milkbottle tops and so on. They're bound to come in useful one day for something.

USA Addresses

AARDVARK ADVENTURES
PO Box 2449
Livermore, CA 94551
(800/388-2687)

CLOTILDE
1909 SW First Ave
Ft. Lauderdale, FL 33315
(305/761-8655)

G STREET FABRICS
11854 Rockville Pike
Rockville, MD 20852
(301/231-8960)

JEHLOR FANTASY FABRICS
730 Andover Park West
Seattle, WA 98188
(206/575-8250)

KEEPSAKE QUILTING
Dover Street
Meredith, NH 03253
(603/279-3351)

NANCY'S NOTIONS
PO Box 683
Beaver Dam, WI
(800/765-0690)

THE PERFECT NOTION
566 Hoyt St.
Darien, CT 06820
(203/968-1257)

TREADLEART
25834 Narbonne Ave, Ste I
Lomita, CA 90717
(800/327-4222)

Costume the World!

To order more copies of this book, send $22.00 ($23.50 for California residents):
Open Chain Publishing, Inc.
PO Box 2634-B
Menlo Park, CA 94026
(415)366-4440
Fax: (415)366-4455
We publish other good books, too, like *Learn Bearmaking, The Busy Woman's Sewing Book, Quick Napkin Creations*, and more.
Send for a free copy of our quarterly newsletter, *The Creative Machine*.
Meanwhile, hug your sewing machine.